W9-BYZ-511

A CONTEMPLATIVE READING OF THE GOSPEL

Luke

The Song of God's Mercy

By Elena Bosetti

Pauline
BOOKS & MEDIA
Boston

Bosetti, Elena.
  [Luca. English]
  Luke : the song of God's mercy / Elena Bosetti.— 1st English ed.
    p. cm.
  Includes bibliographical references.
  ISBN 0-8198-4521-3 (pbk. : alk. paper) 1. Bible. N.T. Luke—Criticism, inter-
pretation, etc. 2. Evangelistic work—Biblical teaching. 3. Evangelistic work—
Catholic Church. I. Title.
  BS2595.52.B6813 2006
  226.4'06—dc22

                              2006001191

The Scripture quotations taken from the Old Testament and contained herein are
from the *New Revised Standard Version Bible: Catholic Edition*, copyright © 1989,
1993, Division of Christian Education of the National Council of the Churches of
Christ in the United States of America. Used by permission. All rights reserved.

Texts of the New Testament used in this work are taken from *The New Testament: St.
Paul Catholic Edition*, translated by Mark A. Wauck, copyright © 2000 by the Society
of St. Paul, Staten Island, New York, and are used by permission. All rights reserved.

Cover design by Rosana Usselmann

Cover art: Saint Luke: Gospels of the Cisoing Abbey, mid-twelfth century, France.
Bridgeman-Giraudon / Art Resource, NY. Bibliotheque Municipale, Lille, France.

All rights reserved. No part of this book may be reproduced or transmitted in any
form or by any means, electronic or mechanical, including photocopying, recording,
or by any information storage and retrieval system without permission in writing
from the publisher.

"P" and PAULINE are registered trademarks of the Daughters of St. Paul.

English language edition arranged through the mediation of Eulama Literary
Agency.

Original edition published in Italian under the title *Luca: Il cammino dell'evangelizzazione.*

Translated by Julia Mary Darrenkamp, FSP

Copyright © 2002 Centro Editoriale Dehoniano, Bologna

First English edition, 2006

Published by Pauline Books & Media, 50 Saint Paul's Avenue, Boston, MA 02130-
3491. www.pauline.org

Printed in the U.S.A.

Pauline Books & Media is the publishing house of the Daughters of St. Paul, an
international congregation of women religious serving the Church with the commu-
nications media.

1 2 3 4 5 6 7 8 9   11 10 09 08 07 06

"…By how he ends, a person becomes known"
(Sir 11:28).

To Mark, who listens to and lives the Word,
and to Maria Grace, John Luke, Damien,
and Gloria, who walk in hope.

Contents

CHAPTER 7

CHAPTER 8

CHAPTER 9

CHAPTER 10

The Gospel of Love 131

Foreword

*T*here is a road that runs through all the regions of the earth, a road that is open in every season of history. It is the road that links Jerusalem to Emmaus and Emmaus to Jerusalem. This road is a symbol, a paradigm, an icon.

All humanity moves along its path. It is an immense caravan of people who are often distrustful or disillusioned, sometimes uncertain or disoriented, but who are always searching or waiting.

Along this road he appears: a mysterious Pilgrim who keeps "company" with two travelers. He approaches and questions them. He comforts and enlightens them. He confronts them and then stops to share a meal with them.

The result? Hearts are warmed and eyes are opened. The road becomes transformed into hope and the journey becomes a joy. And this journey, made together, changes lives and is the beginning of an entirely new story!

This is the "Emmaus story," which Luke recounts almost at the end of his Gospel (24:13–35). The steps taken that afternoon were but the first in a journey that still continues—a journey of meeting and discovery, of conversion and of announcing.

This small book contains a resource that is timely and balanced, competent and warm, reflective and prayerful. It is a gift from the mind and heart of Elena Bosetti, a Sister of Jesus the Good Shepherd (*Pastorelle*), a teacher of Sacred Scripture at the Pontifical Gregorian Institute. This book is a precious pastoral aid that can help us listen to and retell the Gospel today, the "Good News" of Jesus according to the narration of Luke.

In the Book of Acts, Luke seems to be in pursuit of the Word which runs, grows, and diffuses itself (see 12:24). In the Gospel he contemplates the origins, the manifestations, and the effects of this Word, which came to Zechariah in the Temple, to Mary in the house of Nazareth, and to the shepherds on the hills of Bethlehem. It was sung by Elizabeth and Zechariah, by Mary, by the angels, by the shepherds, by Simeon, and by John. Jesus proclaimed it solemnly in the synagogue of Nazareth, and after leaving for Galilee he made it resound in all the cities and villages of Palestine. It was translated into a hymn of joy and was told in the simple stories of the parables.

We still have need of this "Good News." Leading the Church into the third Christian millennium, John Paul II recalled us to the enthusiastic duty of the "new evangelization" (*Tertio Millennio Adveniente,* nos. 11, 57). The Church accepts as an inspiration and as a missionary commitment the call to teach the truth of the Gospel and to give the bread of the Word of God.

"To evangelize," wrote Paul VI, "is the grace and the real vocation of the Church" (*Evangelii Nuntiandi*, no. 14).

The texts from the Gospel of Luke suggested in this volume take us back to the source. In order to announce we need to welcome, and in order to evangelize we need to listen: "Blessed are those who hear the word of God and keep it!" (Lk 11:28) And here we see Mary, the Mother of Jesus, who listens, preserves, and meditates on the Word in her heart (see Lk 2:19, 51; 8:19–21).

Here we also see Mary of Bethany, the attentive disciple sitting at the feet of Jesus (see Lk 10:38–42).

With her *lectio* woven from within the fabric of Luke's narrative, Elena Bosetti manages to draw out, among other things, certain attitudes that are necessary for us today more than ever:

- The desire to question, to inquire. Before setting out on the journey, we need to know the directions, the reason for making the journey, and which road signs we must follow.

- The *joy* of encountering. Only the "company" of the Lord can enflame our hearts and be the source of courage and energy for new and ongoing journeys. The luminous vision of Tabor (Lk 9:28–36) and the tragic one of Calvary (Lk 23:47–49) stand at the beginning of the evangelizing mission of the Church in all times.

- Desire and joy, however, must be translated into *prayer* in order to continue to seek and encounter the Lord.

Speak to us still.
Gather us around you,
like the disciples along the shore of the lake,
or on the mountains, or on the plains;
we are listening for your Gospel.
We want to receive your Word,
even though it be a two-edged sword.
This Word—which is the power of God—
will allow light, love, and the peace that you
    announced
to enter even into our hardened hearts.
Lord, we believe in your Gospel.
Make us worthy of witnessing to it and of
    announcing it.

✠ LORENZO CHIARNELLI
Bishop of Aversa, Italy

CHAPTER I

Were not our hearts burning within us?

*T*he Church of the third millennium is discovering the urgent necessity of a renewed evangelization. In his encyclical letter, *Redemptoris Missio*, which stands in continuity with Paul VI's *Evangelii Nuntiandi*, John Paul II asked Christians to find again the "impetus of the beginnings" with regard to the modern world. Whoever encounters the Risen Lord cannot keep silent and, above all, cannot live as if nothing had happened. It is in this sense that St. Paul proclaims, "Woe to me if I don't proclaim the good news!" (1 Cor 9:16)

Deeply fascinated by the "journey" of the divine Word and by the multiform activity of the Spirit, Luke must have been as impressed with the personality and dedication of the Apostle Paul as he was with Paul's collaborators, both men and women. Faithful companion of the Apostle and his spiritual heir, Luke seems to be the evangelist most suited to the theme of evangelization. His Gospel describes the journey—or rather, the race—of the Good News: first from heaven to earth, then from Jerusalem to Nazareth, and finally from Nazareth back again to Jerusalem, and reaching to the farthest ends of the earth.

Allowing ourselves to be guided by Luke, we want to understand what evangelization really means—what it implies, what it brings about, and what characteristics make up the preaching of Jesus and his disciples, both men and women.

We begin with the icon of the Risen One, who evangelizes his disciples on the road to Emmaus. Here it is important to note that it is not the "Church" that takes the initiative, but the Lord who does so. It is heaven that evangelizes earth. Not by chance do we find angels at the beginning and at the end of the Gospel of Luke. It is they who announce the incarnation and birth of the Savior, and they are the ones who announce the beautiful news of his resurrection from the dead. The Gospel descends from heaven and makes the earth sing. In fact, throughout Luke's Gospel songs of exultation burst forth from the mouths of those who receive joyful news. We will explore these aspects later on.

But Luke is also attentive to the historical journeys and human features of the evangelizers. Therefore, we will also look at some passages dealing with John the Baptist, Simon Peter, and the other itinerant disciples who travel with Jesus, such as Mary of Magdala and her companions.

The evangelizing work of Jesus and his followers follows a path that moves from Galilee, passes through Samaria, and resolutely directs itself toward Jerusalem. Jesus evangelizes in the Temple, the heart of the holy city. For Luke, Jesus evangelizes even after his death, right up to his ascent into heaven.

And so we begin this journey starting at the end (which is the true beginning), listening along the way to words that enflame our heart.

Luke closes his Gospel with the touch of an artist, leaving us an unforgettable scene. The Risen One approaches two disciples on the road to Emmaus and walks beside them, explaining the Scriptures to them until he is joyously recognized. It is a story full of feeling, capable of involving the reader more and more, until he or she can only conclude with the two protagonists: "Weren't our hearts burning within us while he spoke to us on the road, as he opened up the Scriptures to us?" (Lk 24:32)

This story seems particularly suited to helping us approach the Gospel of Luke and begin an itinerary of evangelization in his "school." The perspective that guides the story is the free and selfless gift of the Lord. Here it really is not the Church that draws near to the Risen Lord; it is he himself who crosses the disciples' path and accompanies them on their journey. He is in search of those who have distanced themselves from hope.

The encounter is placed along the road (*en tê hodô*) that stretches from Jerusalem to Emmaus; by the story's end, the road will be taken just as quickly in the opposite direction, from Emmaus to Jerusalem.

The story is told in two principal scenes introduced with the same stylistic formula: "and it happened while" (*ka egeneto en tô*, followed by the infinitive verb):

> *24:15*—and it happened while they were talking and discussing among themselves (*kai egeneto en tô homilein autous*);
>
> *24:30*—and it happened while he was seated at table with them *(kai egeneto en tô kataklithenai auton met'autôn)*.

Here Luke throws into relief the two essential moments of the Christian liturgy: Word and Sacrament, listening to the Scriptures and the Eucharistic liturgy.

Let us allow ourselves to be caught up in the story, as if we were hearing it for the first time.

From Jerusalem to Emmaus

At the beginning of the account the names of the two protagonists are not mentioned, merely that they are "on the way." Luke uses the verb *poreuomai* (to go, to walk, to be on the way), the same verb he uses earlier to describe the journey Jesus makes to Jerusalem and his strong desire to proceed along this way: "...he set his face to go to Jerusalem" (Lk 9:51).

Luke sees the Christian vocation as a way, a journey (*hodos*) that follows the Lord to Jerusalem. So it is significant that the two disciples are leaving Jerusalem behind them. In fact, the two men are going a considerable distance away from the city, around seven miles.

Cleopas (as he is later identified) and his companion have distanced themselves from the holy city and from everything it represents of their disappointed hope. There would be no Messiah, no reconstruction of Israel.... Perhaps the Passover pilgrimage had never seemed like it had that year, so full of a particular expectation. Jesus had "gone up" to Jerusalem, and those who were with him eagerly awaited the fulfillment of the ancient hope.

They had gone up to Jerusalem to sing the song of liberation: tomorrow free in Jerusalem! And instead, everything had ended so soon, so abruptly, before the feast had even taken place. What a tragic Passover!

The Risen One draws near

While they were discussing (*homiloun*) all this among themselves, Jesus "drew near and walked along with them." The Risen One takes the initiative of "drawing near" and of accompanying them on their journey, revealing in this way the gratuitousness of the encounter, together with Luke's particular understanding of the resurrection. The "closeness of the Risen One" is something typical of Luke's Gospel and rather foreign to the viewpoints of Mark and Matthew.

But their eyes are prevented from knowing him

For the disciples to recognize him, it is not enough that Jesus draws near. Simply seeing with the eyes is not enough. Recognizing the Risen One is something that transcends the merely "superficial"; it requires an experience of faith. With the hand of an artist Luke plays with the clearly symbolic contrast between verses 16 and 31:

| (at the beginning) | their eyes were prevented from seeing (v. 16) |
| (at the end) | their eyes were opened (v. 31) |

The journey's beginning is marked by eyes that do not see, as the text says literally: "...their eyes were kept from recognizing him." These eyes will "see" only at the end, after the hearing, the organ of listening, has done all of its work. In fact, the revelation of the Risen One is directed to the ears. Jesus takes the initiative in speaking and introduces himself into the conversation with a question:

"What are these words you are exchanging with each other as you walk?" (v. 17)

This question has a strong effect on the two travelers, who stop short, amazed at the stranger's ignorance of the latest news: "Are you the only person staying in Jerusalem who is unaware of the things that have happened there in these days?" (v. 18) Jesus plays along with them by countering their question with another—"What things?"—thus giving the disciples the chance to explain their thoughts. The result is a resumé of early Christology, as Cleopas and his companion recount the main points of the life of Jesus and the various Passover announcements sprinkled throughout the Gospel of Luke.

First they recall the Master's name and place of origin—"Jesus of Nazareth"—and with that we are taken back to the first two chapters of the Gospel. Then they reminisce about his ministry: "[He] was a prophet mighty in word and deed before God and all the people..." (see Lk 4:32–36; 5:17; 6:19; 7:16; 8:26; 9:19); his death and those responsible for it: "...The chief priests and our rulers handed him over to a sentence of death and had him crucified" (see Lk 23:13–25); the discovery of the empty tomb (see Lk 24:3); and finally the vision of angels and the announcement that Jesus is alive (see Lk 24:4; Ac 25:19).

In the travelers' account are reechoed the various announcements of the resurrection, given respectively by the angels to the women (see Lk 24:6) and by the women to the eleven (see Lk 24:9–10). Also mentioned is the visit of certain disciples to the tomb in order to ascertain the truth of the facts that have been reported (see Lk 24:12–24).

Why are our two travelers not concerned with personally verifying these witnesses of the resurrection? Instead of going on to Emmaus, they should have gone to the tomb to verify what had happened. But Cleopas and his friend were not among those who "lost time" going to the tomb.... Besides, those who went there "did not see him."

We are now at the heart of the story. Jesus listens for some time and eventually takes the floor, going on to reprove the disciples: "How dense you are, and how slow of heart to believe..." the teachings of the Scriptures (vv. 25–27). His question to them is like a refrain often repeated in the Gospel of Luke: "Did not the Messiah have to suffer all these things...?" (see Lk 24:44–46).

The exegesis of the Risen One

The Risen One, who "was a prophet powerful in word," has nothing to say to the disciples except what Moses and all the prophets had written about him, and more precisely about his journey of suffering (v. 26). The Prophet goes back to the prophets. The Risen One becomes an "exegete," and his teaching is the final and supreme exegesis of the Scriptures.

Luke's image of the Risen One explaining the Scriptures reflects a profound truth experienced by the early Church—and in a particular way by Paul—regarding the understanding of Scripture. Sacred Scripture (Old Testament) does not automatically bring with it the understanding of Jesus as the Christ (neither is it true today of the Jewish reading of it). The fact that we're starting from the same beginning (Moses) does not guarantee that we will arrive at the same end (recognizing Jesus as the Messiah). For the early Church, it is the end that explains the beginning. The Risen One is the decisive key, capable of "opening" the Scriptures (Lk 24:32) and of demonstrating the Christological meaning running throughout.

In this light, and contrary to our two protagonists' way of thinking, the passion and death of Jesus do not stand in contradiction with his being the Messiah; instead they reveal him as the authentic Messiah, of whom Moses and the prophets wrote. (The same thing can also be seen in Acts 3:18 and 1 Peter 1:11–12).

"Stay with us...." The Risen One is a guest

The story nears its end. The two disciples have arrived at their destination, but "he walked ahead as if he were going on" (v. 28).

The insistent invitation that Cleopas and his companion extend to the mysterious stranger undoubtedly reflects generous Middle-Eastern hospitality, but something more besides. Here the soul of the Church also shines through in what will become the liturgical invocation of the community:

> "*Stay with us*, because it's near evening...." So he went in to *stay with them* (v. 29).

The Risen One becomes their guest. The hermeneutics of Scripture emphasize the sign of his Passover.

The scene that follows leads us to understand that the two disciples have invited their guest to the place of honor at the table and asked him to pronounce the prayer of blessing over the meal: "...When he reclined at table with them he took the bread and blessed it, broke it, and gave it to them" (v. 30).

Here Jesus performs an ordinary gesture, one that is part of everyday life and custom. To recite the prayer of thanksgiving and to share bread among table companions is in fact the normal function of the head of a family or of a guest. But by now this particular gesture is reminiscent of the Lord's Supper and of his Passover. It is the sign that takes us back to the passion and, significantly, it is actually the act of "breaking the bread" that causes the disciples' eyes to "open" and allows them to recognize the Lord.

What does this connection mean? One important thing to note is that this sign of the Risen One is not a chance occurrence; instead it is a response to the difficulty that the two disciples face, and, even more, a response that goes to the heart of their problem. To recognize the Lord in the act of his death is to find the answer to the difficulty that made them leave Jerusalem in the first place, the answer to the scandal of the passion. "Didn't the Messiah have to suffer all these things...?" the stranger had asked them along the road, thus showing how Scripture would indicate that such a journey was necessary in order for the Messiah to enter into glory. That word is now confirmed in "the breaking of the bread," the sign that takes us back to the liberating death of the Lord (cf. v. 26).

From Emmaus to Jerusalem

The disciples' eyes have good reason to be open. By now they are able to see the two inseparable aspects of the Passover mystery, that is, how death can be the source of life and of glory. Now it is possible for their eyes to open and to see beyond, because the ear and the heart have understood. Faith comes from hearing. It is no wonder then that at the beginning the two travelers were prevented from seeing. To see in faith, which is what we are speaking of here, presupposes a listening to the Word. The

Risen One takes his disciples back to the importance of listening; while they are walking together, he makes the strength of the Word resound again in their hearts. He, the supreme interpreter of the Scriptures, reveals the meaning that pervades it, unravels the mysterious design of salvation that passes through the cross, and by so doing enflames their hearts once again.

As the well-known saying goes, "One can see well only with the heart." Luke seems to agree. Because the heart has understood, the eyes of the disciples are no longer kept from seeing.

But, paradoxically, now that their eyes are opened and the two men are capable of seeing, the Risen One "vanishes" from their sight. Once the disciples' eyes are opened, he disappears. Well, then, was what they experienced simply a vision?

Luke does not actually say that the disciples "saw" Jesus (that is, Luke doesn't employ the verb typically used of an apparition), but that they *"recognized"* him. The moment their eyes are opened, the Risen One is no longer visible because he is not just that traveler, a third person, an "other." The disciples have experienced him alive in their very own life. The sacramental sign allows them and us to "recognize him" not simply as someone outside of ourselves, whom we "can see," but as one who lives in our hearts and warms them, as the living One whom the Church understands as an intimate presence.

Hope is rekindled, along with the strength to get up "that very hour" and return to Jerusalem to recount to the brothers this extraordinary experience. The two disciples come to know the joy of announcing the Good News in the middle of the night, describing how their hearts were enflamed and how they *recognized* him in the breaking of the bread (v. 35; cf. Acts 2:42–46; 20:7–11).

From Jerusalem to Gaza

In the Acts of the Apostles (the second volume of Luke's writings) there is a passage that in many aspects recalls the one just described: it is the encounter of Philip with the Ethiopian (8:26–40).

Again everything takes place along a road. A carriage is coming down from Jerusalem to Gaza, and in the carriage sits a man who is reading aloud. He is an Ethiopian, a eunuch who is an officer of Candace, the Queen of Ethiopia. In Acts the description of the man is exact, but leaves us suspecting that the narrator wants to say something more, perhaps moving to a symbolic level.

The road is one that goes down from the Mediterranean coast where it crosses the Via Maris, a great thoroughfare of international communication connecting Israel to Egypt on one side, and Lebanon to Syria on the other. It is called "the desert road." The absence of rain renders the land parched.

The encounter with the Ethiopian suggests the fulfillment of prophetic words, the universality of the Good News, and the extension of the Christian mission to the very ends of the earth (where perhaps Ethiopia is located).

The fact that the Good News arrives to an Ethiopian eunuch means that this is the end of every exclusion. Even foreigners and those physically disabled or maimed (whom the ancient Law had marginalized) now have free access to divine worship:

> Do not let the foreigner joined to the LORD say,
> "The LORD will surely separate me from his people";
> and do not let the eunuch say,
> "I am just a dry tree."
> For thus says the LORD:
> To the eunuchs who keep my sabbaths,
> who choose the things that please me
> and hold fast my covenant,
> I will give, in my house and within my walls,
> a monument and a name
> better than sons and daughters;
> I will give them an everlasting name
> that shall not be cut off (Isa 56:3–5).

From Word to sacrament

On their way to Emmaus the two disciples discuss among themselves events regarding the passion and death of Jesus. On his journey the Ethiopian reads Isaiah 53, that is, the prophecy of the passion of the Servant of the Lord.

What follows in each story is that a "stranger" appears: Jesus in the Gospel of Luke and Philip in Acts. In both accounts the stranger "questions" the person(s) to whom he is speaking and "interprets" the Scriptures from a Christological perspective (see Ac 8:29–35).

In each case we have an extended narrative ending in a sacramental sign: the two disciples ask Jesus to "stay with them"; the eunuch asks to "be baptized" (see Ac 8:36–38). The stories end respectively in the breaking of bread and in baptism, the two fundamental sacraments of Christian initiation.

The conclusion of both stories indicates an "absence" coupled with profound joy. In the Gospel account, Jesus disappears from the sight of the two disciples, and with hearts full of joy they make their return journey to Jerusalem. As for Philip, he is carried off by the Spirit, and the eunuch continues his journey "rejoicing."

In this we see outlined what evangelization means for Luke's community!

CHAPTER 2

Heaven evangelizes earth

At the beginning and at the end of Luke's Gospel we encounter the figure of angels. They announced the resurrection of the Crucified to the women returning to the tomb, as the disciples of Emmaus later testified (Lk 24:4–7, 22–23); angels also announced the birth of John and of Jesus (Lk 1—2). So both the coming of the Savior into this world and his resurrection from the dead directly involve messengers from heaven. Once more we see that evangelization begins from on high; it is the work of God himself.

Undoubtedly, as can be seen in the preceding reading, the first move is made by the Risen One, who accompanies the two desolate travelers and who, along the way, warms their hearts with his interpretation of the Scriptures. Thus he enables his disciples and the whole community to read the events of his passion, death, and resurrection in the light of Scripture, since ultimately it is about him that Moses, the prophets, and the psalms speak.

This unique evangelizing activity of the Risen One, this awareness that Jesus is Lord and the fulfillment of Scripture, opens the way to the announcement of the Gospel or, to put it in Luke's words, the preaching of "repentance and forgiveness of sins for all nations...starting from Jerusalem" (Lk 24:47; cf. Ac 1:8).

But Luke is equally aware of the routes leading to this culminating point and of the ways in which they converge. He goes back to the *arché*, that is, to the beginning of evangelization, presenting us with the ministry of John the Baptist and then that of Jesus and his disciples. But not satisfied with this, Luke carefully traces the course of events back even further, until he reaches their source: the *anothen*, the beginnings. And at both the beginning and the end of his narrative we discover that the joyful announcement transcends earth and human protagonists; heaven is involved, and angels are at work.

Announcement to the priest Zechariah

The first time Luke uses the verb "to evangelize" (*euangelizomai*), he does so to describe the duty of an angel. We are at the first scene of the Gospel, which takes place in the Temple of Jerusalem. Zechariah is an elderly priest of the class of Abia, and it is his turn to offer incense.

The opportunity to offer the sacrifice of incense by turn happened rarely, perhaps only once in a priest's life. The moment is therefore one of great spiritual intensity. The Book of Exodus prescribes that Aaron burn fragrant incense "every morning when he dresses the lamps," and again "when [he] sets up the lamps in the evening, he shall offer it" (Ex 30:7–8). It was probably sunset when Zechariah entered the Holy of holies to make the offering (the angel Gabriel also chose this moment to reveal himself to the prophet Daniel: see Dan 9:21). Those who were gathered in the respective courts of men and women were praying. And behold, "an angel of the Lord appeared to him, standing to the right of the incense altar" (Lk 1:11).

The angel's message is articulated in seven points: your prayer was heard; your wife will have a son; you will call him John; you will have joy and gladness; many others will rejoice at his birth; he will be great in the sight of the Lord and will be a Nazarite, that is, he will not drink wine but will be filled with the Holy Spirit from his mother's womb; he will turn many people of Israel to the Lord their God, going before him with the spirit and power of Elijah.

The accent on the Christological dimensions of this message is striking: from the very beginning of this announcement the figure of John is already completely oriented toward the Lord Jesus.

The angel's first affirmation seems somewhat enigmatic. What prayer has been heard? The text does not speak of Zechariah having made a special prayer, although it presupposes one. From the moment he began offering the official Temple sacrifice it is logical to suppose that Zechariah was praying on behalf of the people. Some exegetes have suggested that the old priest prayed for a son rather than for the good of the people, but verse 18 discourages such an interpretation. How could he have prayed for the birth of a son when he was well aware that such a thing was by now impossible? "I am elderly," Zechariah objects, "and my wife is advanced in years."

Therefore, the angel was either referring to the hearing of a prayer Zechariah had made in the past, or else was introducing a new prospect: the prayer for the good of the people is actually realized through the gift of a son who will bring Israel back to the Lord. In other words, God heard both the ministerial prayer of his priest and at the same time the prayer which the priest no longer dared to pray or even to hope for (the birth of a son), showing that between the two realities there was a strict connection: what was good for Zechariah would also be for the good of the people.

> "Fear not, Zechariah—your petition has been heard. Your wife Elizabeth will bear you a son, and you shall name him John" (Lk 1:13).

Joy will follow humiliation—an intimate joy, a domestic joy, but one that is also for all the people: "many will rejoice at his birth" (Lk 1:14).

Zechariah cannot quite convince himself that such can be true. He asks for an explanation: "How will this happen? For I am an old man, and my wife is getting on in years." His objection meets with the sign of silence in return. When God speaks it is better that one keep quiet... (cf. Lk 1:19–20).

The scene proceeds quickly to its conclusion. From the Temple, the lofty place of worship, we move immediately to a house where we find Elizabeth, the protagonist of this maternal annunciation, at the center:

> After these days his wife Elizabeth became pregnant, and she secluded herself for five months, saying, "Thus has the Lord dealt with me in the days he deigned to take away my disgrace before men" (Lk 1:24–25).

To remain hidden in order to contemplate

Here Luke turns and surprises us with his subtlety. Why does Elizabeth, freed from the shame of sterility, hide herself from public view? Why this escape from the eyes of others, especially of the curious? Is she embarrassed at being pregnant at her advanced age? Is she simply trying to avoid unwelcome remarks? If such were the case, it would be logical to expect the concealment to last for the duration of her pregnancy, or at least during the latter months rather than "immediately," as the text instead suggests: "Elizabeth conceived, and for five months she remained in seclusion."

The reason for her seclusion appears to be altogether different than what one might expect; Elizabeth kept herself hidden in order to contemplate. When God speaks it is right that one keep silent (Zechariah remained mute); when God works marvels it is not right to lose oneself in chatter, but to immerse oneself in religious silence. And so this scene ends as it had begun: before God (see Lk 1:8).

Elizabeth retires from public view to remain totally beneath the gaze of God, who has decided to rest the divine gaze upon her. The mother of the precursor precedes the mother of the Savior in her confession of praise (*confessio laudis*), in her joyous recognition of the marvels that the Lord has accomplished for her:

> "This is what the Lord has done for me when he looked favorably on me and took away the disgrace I have endured among my people" (Lk 1:25).

The annunciation to Mary of Nazareth

Six months after the joyful announcement to Zechariah, the angel Gabriel is sent by God with a message that has no precedent in the history of salvation. The Old Testament knows the experience of the sterile made fruitful, but the wonder of the virginal conception is in fact totally unheard of.

In many respects the annunciation to Mary of Nazareth parallels that to Zechariah, but it is important to see how they unfold at different levels.

Coming into her presence

Luke sets the scene at Nazareth, which at the time was a small and beautiful village surrounded by the mountains of Galilee. Mary is imagined probably at home; in fact, the text describes the movement of the angel as an entrance: "And when he came into her presence..."

Iconography has familiarized us with Mary of Nazareth at prayer during the annunciation. Some artists have painted her with the book of the psalms in her hands, in an attitude of listening and of communion with the

Lord. The text actually says nothing about this; it refers only to the greeting of the angel. And strangely enough, the angel does not pronounce Mary's name in greeting, but calls her "full of grace." It is almost as if Mary receives a new name, a new identity:

"Hail, full of grace, the Lord is with you!"

The word "grace" (*charis*) indicates the merciful love of the Lord, his benevolence. Mary is full of this benevolence. She is filled with the divine love; she wholly accepts and corresponds to it. The angel's greeting recalls the joyful announcement that the prophet Zephaniah earlier directed to the city of Jerusalem, represented as a feminine persona: "Daughter of Zion."

Zeph 3:14–17	*Lk 1:26–28*
Sing aloud, O daughter Zion... *Rejoice...* O daughter Jerusalem!	"*Hail,* full of grace,
The king of Israel, *the* LORD, *is in your midst...*	*the Lord is with you!*
Do not fear, O Zion;	*Fear not,* Mary— you have found grace before the Lord.
...The LORD, your God, is *in your midst,* a warrior who gives victory...	And, behold, you will conceive *in your womb* and bear a son, and you shall name him Jesus" (= Savior).

Behold, you will conceive in your womb

The words of the angel announce a maternity by the
work of the Holy Spirit. And so Mary is placed, in an
imminent way, in direct contact with the Author of life,
the God from whom every paternity and maternity has its
origin. Her child will be the "son of a woman" (Gal 4:4)
and the Son of God, son of the Most High!

Mary herself will have the responsibility of giving him
a very symbolic name: Jesus (Savior), a responsibility
which Matthew attributes to Joseph (see Mt 1:21). And so
is accomplished what God had promised to David
through the prophet Nathan, that is, a throne will be
established which is stable and secure, a "house," a reign
without end, based on a most profound reciprocity: "I will
be his father, and he will be my son."

A synoptic reading with Second Samuel 7:12–14
shows surprising points of similarity:

2 Sam 7:12–14	*Lk 1:32–33*
I will be a father to him, and he shall be a *son* to me...	"He will be called *Son* of the Most High,
I will establish the *throne* of his kingdom forever.	and the Lord God will give him the *throne* of his father David.
Your *house* and your	He will reign over the *house* of Jacob forever,
kingdom shall be made sure forever...	and his *kingdom* will have no end."

Mary's objection: How is this possible?

Mary realizes that God is turning her plans upside-down. She is the promised spouse of Joseph, a man of the house of David. But until now she has not had with him (nor with others) any sexual relations. It is in this sense that she says: "I do not know man."

In the narrative, Mary's objection—"How will this come about, since I do not know man?"—serves to advance the story; it prepares the climate needed to welcome the heart of the message embodied in the angel's reply. In any case, the tradition of the Church interprets these words as indicating that Mary had an implicit personal project: she is a virgin and intends to remain so, thus excluding herself from every Hebrew woman's dream to become if not the mother then at least an ancestor of the Messiah. This interpretation was most likely not the result of later ascetical practices, as some would have it. On the contrary, subsequent practices have arisen on the basis of Mary's choice and the example of Jesus.

From such a standpoint Mary's words would take on this meaning: *What about my promise to the Lord to remain a virgin? How can what you tell me be possible given what I have promised to offer to the Lord?* The angel Gabriel reassures her: "The Holy Spirit will come upon you, and the power of the Most High will overshadow you" (Lk 1:35).

More than explaining the mystery, these words highlight the faith of the young woman of Nazareth, who is invited to entrust herself totally to God. Nothing is impossible to God. She will be like the Ark of the Covenant: full of the divine presence, enwrapped in the fertile power of God.

Certain similarities with Exodus 40:34 are noteworthy:

Ex 40:34	*Lk 1:35*
Then the cloud covered the *tent* of meeting,	"The power of the Most High will overshadow *you;*
and the glory of the LORD filled the *tabernacle.*	therefore, the holy child to be born will be called Son of God."

The sign given to Mary

Gabriel also leaves a "sign" with Mary. Another woman, her cousin Elizabeth, has experienced the grace of the Lord. Everyone had called Elizabeth "sterile," but now she, like the aged Sarah, has been saved from her humiliation and is expecting a child.

The sign is given in order to show the power of the Most High and consequently to sustain Mary's faithful adherence to his word. The refrain that unites the stories of Sarah and of Elizabeth is in fact the same: "Nothing is impossible with God."

Gen 18:9–14	*Lk 1:36–37*
"...Your wife Sarah...	"And, behold, your kinswoman Elizabeth,
shall have a son..." [Sarah:] "After I have grown old,	even she conceived a son
and my husband is old...."	in her old age...

It had ceased to be with Sarah after the manner of women.	And this is the sixth month for her who was called barren.
The LORD said: "Is anything too wonderful for the LORD?"	For nothing is impossible with God."

Mary's consent

Mary responds with an unconditional yes; she places all her trust in the Lord: "Here I am, the servant of the Lord; let it be with me according to your word." Hers is the obedience of faith.

Here I am! Mary does not restrict herself to offering some *thing;* she offers herself. In that "Here I am," she gives everything she is: her freedom, her enthusiasm. She wants only one thing—what pleases the Lord. Mary has offered her virginity in love, and for love here she is, totally available to a project that surpasses her and yet at the same time involves her.

Mary puts everything in this "giving of herself." She considers herself "the *servant* of the Lord." This is the title that best describes her, as is well expressed in her *Magnificat:* "He has looked with favor on the lowliness of his *servant.*" This title of "servant" constitutes a new theology of great significance. Of her alone among women is it said that she is "the servant of the Lord." In a feminine way Mary is the servant of YHWH spoken of by the prophets—above all in Second Isaiah—and that in the New Testament refers to Jesus. The mother of the Messiah is in perfect spiritual harmony with the ideal of obedience that Jesus will live. She is mother above all in the obedience of faith.

The fact that God has exalted her does not diminish her humility in the least, but rather reinforces it. Mary is the obedient servant reaching out completely to her Lord.

Announcement to the shepherds

The Gospel brought by the angels arrives progressively to a man, then a woman, and finally to a group of people, the shepherds. The subject matter of this third announcement is the birth of the Messiah.

It is not without reason that the angel of the Lord chooses to appear to shepherds rather than other possible audiences. A thousand years earlier in similar camps David had pastured his father's sheep. And it was precisely at Bethlehem that the prophet Samuel consecrated him as king: from a shepherd of sheep, David became shepherd of Israel.

Now at the time when Jesus was born, the prestige enjoyed by shepherds was over. Official Judaism had marginalized them because of their lifestyle. Their trade was discouraged and even looked upon with suspicion: shepherds openly transgressed the Sabbath rest and went to the synagogue infrequently, since they had to lead the flock to pasture also on the Sabbath. Shepherds were therefore unpopular with the heads of official Judaism; they were kept at a distance and judged with a certain disdain as "people of the earth," who walked in the darkness, far from the Law of the Lord.

> There were shepherds in the same region, living out of doors and keeping guard at night over their flock. An angel of the Lord appeared to them and the glory of the Lord shone around them, and they were greatly afraid. And the angel said to them, "Fear not! for behold, I bring you good news [*euangelizomai*] which will give joy to the whole nation, because this day a savior has been born for you in the city of David who is the Messiah, the Lord" (Lk 2:8–11).

As in the first two annunciations, to Zechariah and to the Virgin of Nazareth, the shepherds are here invited above all not to be afraid. This visit from heaven is not a prediction of judgment or of misfortune; on the contrary, the messenger is the bearer of great joy, which involves the shepherds in a direct way (and here Luke shows his personal preferences), but which will be equally a joy for all people.

The long-awaited One has arrived; he is born today and is truly for them a Savior, the Christ. The words of this extraordinary annunciation seem well chosen. In particular there resounds a word articulated throughout the pages of the third Gospel—today, this day (*semeron*): "This day is born," the angels announce to the shepherds; "Today this word has been fulfilled," proclaims Jesus at Nazareth; "Today salvation has come to this house," he declares to Zacchaeus; "Today you will be with me in paradise," he promises to the crucified thief who had asked to be remembered. The *today* of the Gospel of Luke emphasizes the contemporaneousness of salvation and its inescapable presence.

Three titles describe the newborn child: *Soter* ("Savior"); *Christos* ("Messiah"); and *Kyrios* ("Lord") (see Lk 2:11). It is not just any Savior who is announced by the angels, but the long-awaited One, the eschatological Savior, Christ the Lord.

What to a superficial reader might seem like nothing more than a curious detail—"You will find a child, swaddled and lying in a manger"—in the eyes of believers takes on the paradoxical characteristics of divine love: "though he was rich he became poor for your sake so that he might enrich you by his poverty" (2 Cor 8:9).

In closing, we can observe the behavior of the shepherds. They prefigure the pastoral minister who develops the work of evangelization. The shepherds leave without delay, going to the place indicated, and after having seen the child, they tell the story of him to everyone. "And all who heard were amazed at what the shepherds told them" (Lk 2:18). They go, they see, and they return to announce—exactly like the women on the morning of the resurrection.

The Fathers of the Church did not hesitate to distinguish a unique correspondence between the shepherds of Bethlehem and the pastors of evangelization, as this splendid homily of Pseudo-Epiphanius attests:

> Be attentive to the facts and acclaim the marvels that accompany the twofold birth of Christ.

An angel announced to Mary the birth of Christ from a mother, and an angel also announced to Mary Magdalen his rebirth from the sepulcher.

By night Christ was born at Bethlehem, and it is also by night that he was born again in Zion.

In swaddling clothes he was wrapped at his birth, and also here [in Zion] he was wrapped in bands.

A place [he had] at Bethlehem, in the manger; but also in the tomb [he found] a place, almost a manger.

The shepherds, first among many, announced the birth of the Christ; but the shepherd-disciples of Christ were also the first among many to announce the rebirth of Christ from the dead. [...]

If you consider these things as if they were fantasy and do not listen to them with the ears of faith, the seals of the sepulcher of Christ, which remained intact at his rebirth from the dead, will accuse you. In fact, as Christ was born of the Virgin, leaving intact the seals at the gate of her virgin nature [...] in the same way the rebirth of Christ came about without opening the seals of the tomb (*Homily II for Holy Saturday*, PG 43, 441–444).

CHAPTER 3

The Gospel liberates song

*T*he Good News that comes down from heaven causes movement on earth, puts events in motion, and inspires songs to well up. In this *lectio* we will pause at length over the canticles—scattered like stars in the first two chapters of Luke—as responses of praise that describe the welcoming of the Gospel.

Elizabeth's song

In the house of Zechariah, as later in the Cenacle (cf. Ac 2:1–4), everyone is filled with the Holy Spirit: not only John, as the angel Gabriel had announced, but his mother also is "full of the Holy Spirit," and finally so is Zechariah. It is the fullness of the Holy Spirit that gives rise to prophecy and song.

The first one to sing is Elizabeth:

"Blessed are you among women, and blessed is the fruit of your womb!" (Lk 1:42)

Her song is an explosion of joy and prophecy, a surprising acclamation to the "mother of *my* Savior." This means that Elizabeth not only perceived in Mary the sign and the heartbeat of a new life; she also grasped the nature of this maternity that did not have precedence, the birth of the Messiah. Mary is acclaimed mother of that Lord whom Elizabeth, too, acknowledges in faith: "my Lord."

"For, behold, when the sound of your greeting came to my ears, the baby in my womb leapt with a great joy. Blessed is she who believed that there would be a fulfillment of what was spoken to her by the Lord" (Lk 1:44–45).

The ark of the new covenant has come into Elizabeth's home and she, like David before her, proclaims herself unworthy of such a visit:

2 Sam 6:9	*Lk 1:43*
"How can the ark of the LORD come into my care?"	"But how is it that the mother of my Lord should come to me?"

And, like David, Elizabeth too praises and blesses:

"Blessed are you among women, and blessed is the fruit of your womb!" (Lk 1:42)

In her admirable canticle, Elizabeth shows where Mary's true greatness lies. She attests to what the Spirit, and not mere human vision, is able to see. This is the eminent value of Mary's faith and obedience:

"Blessed is she who believed that there would be a fulfillment of what was spoken to her by the Lord" (Lk 1:45).

The mother of the precursor is therefore the first to proclaim blessed, *makaria*, the mother of the Messiah; she is the first to pronounce a beatitude destined to be welcomed and repeated by "every generation" (Lk 1:48).

Now it is Mary's turn to speak. The sign given to her by Gabriel has been confirmed; her elderly cousin, who was thought to be barren, is the next to give birth, "because nothing is impossible to God."

Mary's canticle

It is to God that Mary addresses praises of her own maternity. Her *psyche* ("soul, life") and her *pneuma* ("spirit") reach out toward the Lord in an uncontainable joy, because he has looked upon the lowliness of his servant and has worked marvels for her.

The movement of the Magnificat

The canticle is directed in two ways, one vertical and the other horizontal. The ascending movement deals with the relationship between Mary and her Lord, and the horizontal movement is situated within a humble and believing people.

These movements could be likened to two stanzas, so closely connected that the second is almost a prolongation of the first. It is here that we actually find the "reasons" for the canticle, expressed by the double "because" or "for" (*hoti*). There is no explicit link given in the passage between the first and second stanzas, almost as if its absence points out the connection between an event placed on the first level (the maternity of Mary) and its historical and communitarian foundation: the mercy shown toward every generation, the assistance given to Israel. This connection is specified in the concluding formula: "As [*kathos*] he spoke to our fathers" (Lk 1:55), thus interpreting the series of saving actions in view of the promises made to the patriarchs.

The servant of the Lord

Mary's canticle leaves Elizabeth, Zechariah, their house, the neighbors, and every other particular completely in the shadows. At the center of the scene there is only she, the mother-servant of the Lord, completely turned toward him.

Mary's song ascends to the Lord from whom everything descends. It rises up to the Almighty who has deigned to look upon his handmaid, renewing for her the wonders of the exodus.

The *ascending movement* of the Magnificat responds to the *descending movement* of the Lord: "He has looked with favor on the lowliness of his servant." Mary's very life rises up in song because the glance of the Most High has bent down to her. Mary is aware of being, so to speak, at the center of attention: on the part of God, who has looked precisely on her, and on the part of humanity, "All generations will call me blessed." But in "being at the center" she remains completely detached. She is there only in order to proclaim the wonders of the Lord.

The servant among the poor ones of the Lord

The scene expands. While generations rise up and call her blessed, Mary seems almost to disappear within a multitude moving in the same direction as she. That multitude is made up of those who fear the Lord, on whom is bestowed—as on her—the Almighty's mercy. They are the crowds of the small and the poor, a humble people.

Further on, the scene becomes even more populated. On one side of the stage there are the proud, the powerful, and the rich. On the opposite side there are the humble, the hungry, and the homeless, those who fear and trust in the One who alone is powerful. The great works accomplished by the Lord in favor of his servant, raised up from *tapeinosis* (her "lowliness," in the sense of poverty and humility), are repeated with impressive force for all the *tapeinoi* ("the lowly"), the poor and humble of the earth, the true descendents of Abraham. Mary's song is now their song. She and they praise and dance together, as on the shores of the Red Sea.

The paradigm of the Exodus

In effect, the Magnificat re-echoes the song of the other Mary: Miriam, the sister of Moses, the prophetess who took up tambourines and intoned the hymn of praise to God the savior. It is God who "has done" wonders, turning roles and situations upside down.

In this regard, one cannot escape the relevance of the given reading. The verb *epoiesen* ("he has done") is used twice in the Magnificat: first in relation to Mary—"He has done great things for me" (Lk 1:49)—and second in emphatic positions at the beginning of verse 50, where the sevenfold action in favor of Israel is introduced:

> He has shown strength...
> He has scattered the proud...
> He has brought down the powerful...
> He has lifted up the lowly...
> He has filled the hungry with good things...
> He has sent the rich away empty...
> He has helped his servant Israel.

Seven precise actions, indicative of something full and complete (symbolized by the number seven in the Bible).

The initial expression, "he has shown the strength of his arm," is clearly evocative of the Exodus, when YHWH manifested his power against the Pharaoh's arrogance. Furthermore, the last action of the series mentions Israel, the object of God's affectionate mercy, helped by God because of his faithfulness to Abraham and to his promise.

The scene in Exodus is laid out with sharp clarity. On the banks of the Red Sea the prophetess and sister of Moses and Aaron, the only "Mary" of whom the Old Testament speaks, dances and praises the victory of the Lord:

> "Sing to the LORD, for he has triumphed gloriously;
> horse and rider he has thrown into the sea" (Ex 15:21).

This song is echoed on the edge of the New Testament by Mary of Nazareth, celebrating the events of which she has been made the protagonist:

"My soul gives praise to the Lord....
For the Mighty One has done great things for me....
He has shown might with his arm....
He has pulled down the mighty from their thrones,
and exalted the lowly..." (Lk 1:47, 49, 51–52).

God's work in Mary does not merely correspond to his saving action in the past, to the consistent divine behavior, but consists much more in the accomplishment of the promises made to the patriarchs. This is not therefore just any work inserted among many, but the fulfillment and summit of them all.

The golden thread of mercy

The Magnificat sings the story of divine mercy, which bestows itself in many forms: toward the mothers of Israel and toward their sons, in fidelity to the promise made to their father Abraham, in whose name the canticle closes. Mercy, the divine *eleos*, is therefore the guiding theme of the Magnificat, the golden thread that connects Mary's situation to that of Israel. It is not by chance that the ending of the Magnificat contains two points that are structurally relevant: verse 50, which serves as a bridge between Mary's personal situation and that of the community, and verse 54, at the end of the sevenfold salvation of Israel:

"And his *mercy* is from generation to generation toward those who fear him" (v. 50).
"He has come to the aid of his servant, Israel, mindful of his *mercy*" (v. 54).

Zechariah will speak of mercy as well, when, full of the Holy Spirit, his tongue is loosened and he bursts into a song of praise and blessing.

The Canticle of Zechariah

The *Benedictus* is the canticle of the Old Testament flowing into the New, the hymn of hope fulfilled because the God of Israel has visited and redeemed his people. Here our priest resembles a prophet or poet; the hesitation he had expressed in the Temple now gives way to straightforward praises that are almost explosive in force. Like Mary before him, Zechariah addresses himself directly to the Lord, the God of Israel. And like the Virgin, he immediately explains the reasons for his praise:

> "Blessed be the Lord God of Israel—he has visited and set his people free" (Lk 1:68).

In the canticle of Zechariah the idea of salvation builds toward a crescendo that begins with liberation "from our enemies and from the hand of all who hate us" (v. 71) and culminates in the "forgiveness of their sins" (v. 77). In all probability, at the foundation of this progressive line of development is the idea of liberation from political enslavement. But from the perspective of Lucan editing, the theme seems already spiritualized: enemies are those who make attempts on a person's "life," understood in all its fullness and depth. In this sense, verses 74–75 positively affirm the service of God in holiness and righteousness, and verse 77 internalizes the concept of liberation, speaking of "forgiveness of their sins."

Verse 72 is the driving force of the canticle. The praises are returned to their center and heart, where mercy and faithfulness are united. The *Benedictus* proclaims that the "reason" for the visitation of the God of Israel is in order for God to "be merciful." God does not remember the reasons that would hasten judgment, because he remembers his mercy.

The visit of the sun from on high and the way of peace

The waiting that was declared accomplished is not completely over. Zechariah closes his canticle by looking forward, toward the coming that will touch his son: the visit of the sun which rises from on high.

Through experience we know the sun that rises from below. Even Egyptian sun worship sings of the sun's daily struggle to climb the horizon after confronting great difficulties in its voyage through the subterranean ocean. For love of humanity the sun rises every morning; it is the reawakening of creation and the resurrection of life. The sun of which Zechariah sings rises and at the same time descends. It rises "from on high" and so really "descends." Once again heaven descends and embraces the earth.

The light of the eastern star puts shadows to flight, enlightens those who sleep, and finally awakens them. The quiet of the night gives way to the movement of the new day. A path emerges from the darkness—a way which at first seems hazy and vague, but then little by little becomes more pronounced. On this path John embarked alone, but he hasn't remained alone. Many have followed him, ready to allow themselves to be evangelized and converted.

The canticle of the angels

In the Gospel, a few meager words describe the birth of a God who, for love of human beings, made himself a pilgrim of love and of peace. His crib was a manger for animals; his parents simply were not able to find anything better. For him there was no "place." In any event, that night—for the first time in the Gospel of Luke—it was heaven itself, rather than human beings, which bothered to sing God's praises.

> And, suddenly, with the angel was an assembly of the heavenly host, praising God and saying, "Glory to God in high heaven, and, on earth, peace to those in whom he is pleased" (Lk 2:13–14).

A canticle in miniature, there are no verbs in this last verse, and their absence is often interpreted with the sense of a fervent greeting: Glory to God in the highest! But in the song of the angels, glory and peace are not exactly being invoked; they are not a mere greeting (Let there be glory! Let there be peace!). Neither are they songs of prophecy (There will be peace). Instead, they are proclaimed as a reality that is in fact present and has already been accomplished.

With the birth of Jesus, God has accomplished glory in the highest heavens and peace on earth. God himself glorifies his name, working salvation and bringing peace to the earth, and not simply in the heavens...

In this sense the song that is sung by the angels is diametrically distanced from the one that men and women will later sing when Jesus, welcomed as the Messiah, enters Jerusalem. In that circumstance, the whole crowd of disciples began to praise God in a loud voice, saying:

"Blessed is the king who comes in the name of the Lord; peace in heaven and glory in the highest!" (Lk 19:38)

Here it is curious to note that those who "proclaim" are living on earth but thinking of heaven; the peace and glory of which they speak are situated in heaven: "in the heavens peace and glory in the highest" (only Luke records this expression). Instead, when Jesus is born, the angels—that is, the inhabitants of heaven—sing of "peace on earth"!

Perhaps we have not taken the song of the angels seriously enough. We may have repeated the same words— glory and peace—but applied them to the wrong place, lifting our hands and proclaiming the peace of heaven like the crowds of Jerusalem. But Christmas tells us that peace has already descended to the earth. It only needs to take root and flourish through men and women who welcome the love of the Lord in their lives.

The canticle of Simeon

Now, in the symbolic setting of the Temple, the heart of Jerusalem, Luke places two types of figures, a man and a woman full of the Holy Spirit. The first to arrive on the

scene is Simeon, "an upright and devout man who awaited the liberation of Israel" (Lk 2:25).

Awaiting "consolation" is what mainly characterizes
this venerable gentleman; he incarnates the great hope
that animates Israel: the awaiting of messianic consolation
(cf. Is 40:1; 49:13; 52:9).

We cannot allow the accentuated place given the Holy
Spirit to pass unobserved. The term *pneuma* (spirit) recurs
three times in Simeon's presentation: *the Spirit of God* rest-
ed on him; *the Spirit* revealed to him (that he would not
die before he had seen the Anointed of the Lord), and
finally, *guided by the Spirit,* he went into the Temple.

The elderly Simeon shows that he is familiar with
God's world and allows himself to be guided by the Spirit.
We are not surprised then when a song bursts forth from
his lips. Simeon sings with the joy of eyes that now see;
eyes that, fulfilled in having seen that for which they
ardently longed, can now close:

> "Now you send your servant away in peace, O Master,
> according to your word, because my eyes have seen your
> salvation prepared in the presence of all peoples, a light of
> revelation to the Gentiles and glory to your people Israel"
> (Lk 2:29–32).

Simeon's eyes see in Jesus the light that is destined to
shine before the faces of the pagans: "Then the glory of the
Lord shall be revealed, and all people shall see it together"
(Isa 40:5). This light will expand over all the earth—before
all people—and it will be the supreme glory of Israel.

Anna, the woman of praise

Unlike Simeon, who came to the Temple by circumstance, moved by the Holy Spirit, the prophetess Anna was already in the holy place. Luke describes her in a detailed manner: she is the daughter of Phanuel (which recalls Penuel, "the face of God": Gen 32:31); she belongs to the tribe of Asher and is a widow of advanced age, "having lived seven years with her husband from her virginity and alone as a widow up to eighty-four years" (Lk 2:36–37).

The Temple has become her home—"she never left the Temple"—not merely from a logistical point of view, but also and above all as a spiritual abode. Anna has made praising God the meaning and the reason of her daily life.

While Simeon was not designated as a prophet but prophesied all the same, Anna is called "the prophetess." She is a prophetess, however, who keeps silent. Perhaps her prophecy coincides with the simple fact of her being present here at this moment as a woman who witnesses, who with her presence confirms Simeon's prophetic words.

For Luke, this woman incarnates praise: "She began to praise God" in the manner of the prophetess Miriam, the sister of Moses, who at the beautiful age of ninety celebrated with surprisingly youthful energy the work of salvation accomplished by the Lord (cf. Ex 15:20).

But there is more. Anna undertakes a clear work of evangelization, as the disciples of Jesus will later do in the radiant days after the resurrection (cf. Lk 24:1–11). Like the shepherds of Bethlehem, Anna proceeds to speak to everyone of Jesus:

> She spoke about him to all who were awaiting the liberation of Israel (Lk 2:38).

Perhaps this is the principal reason why Luke doesn't hesitate to describe her as "the prophetess." Grown old in fasting and prayer, the widow Anna steps beyond the threshold of the Old Testament; she is already standing in the New. Her prophecy is an enthusiastic word about Jesus to all who are waiting for redemption.

CHAPTER 4

John, the precursor and evangelizer

*I*n the Gospel of Luke no masculine figure has a position of prominence like John—not even Peter, the first of the apostles. Obviously the early Church must have had a profound awareness of John's greatness.

Jesus' fascination with John

The mission of Jesus finds its beginnings in his encounter with John and with John's work of evangelization. Although it isn't explicitly stated, most likely Jesus first listened to the preaching of the Baptist before going into the water of the Jordan to be baptized like all the other people.

John must have had a strong impact on Jesus. One could say that he was Jesus' "vocationist," the man who sparked the decisive turning point of Jesus' life: the passage from private sphere to the public activity of a preacher and healer.

All the Gospels give great importance to the ministry of the Baptist, but Luke paints the figure in more vibrant colors. John is the precursor, the evangelizer of the people, and above all the prophet-bridge between the old and the new, between the period of Israel and that of Jesus (cf. Lk 16:16).

Beginning with the baptism of John

For Mark everything begins with the kerygmatic announcement of John the Baptist. This marks the *arche*, the beginning and foundation of the Gospel. Nothing is said of that which comes before. The beginning coincides with the cry of the voice in the desert calling for penance and conversion (cf. Mk 1:4–5).

At first glance it might appear that Luke thinks differently than Mark. In fact, immediately after Luke's prologue he doesn't bring us into the desert, where the powerful voice of John resounds, but instead brings us to the heart of the Temple, where the elderly Zechariah is officiating.

But, looking more closely, the preaching of John also constitutes the *arche*, or the beginning, for Luke. This is clearly seen in the Acts of the Apostles, where the baptism of John is established as the "beginning":

"Therefore, one of those men who accompanied us the whole time the Lord Jesus came and went among us—*beginning with [arxamenos]* the baptism of John, right up to the day he was taken from us—must become with us a witness to his resurrection" (1:21–22).

The "beginning" designated by the early Church, therefore, is the baptism of John.

John's prophetic vocation

The first part of the passage (Lk 3:1–6) places the vocation of John in a political and religious context. With a broad expression that has no equal in the Gospel except in the prologue, Luke creates a notable break and new beginning in his narration. First of all, he offers the historical-political coordinates of the Roman Empire (Tiberius was emperor, Pontius Pilate was procurator of Judea, Philip was ruler of Iturea and Traconitus, and Lysanius was ruler of Abilene) and political-religious indications concerning Israel (it was during the high priesthood of Annas and Caiaphas). And so, in a solemn form and with the clear stamp of the Old Testament, the evangelist presents the eruption of the word of God:

> The word of God came to John son of Zechariah in the desert (Lk 3:2).

On the one hand this presentation connects the figure of John to the prophets of the Old Testament and to Abraham himself, and emphasizes the absolute freedom of the divine initiative: the Word of God came to Abraham (Gen 15:1), Elijah (1 Kings 18:31), Jeremiah (Jer 1:2), Ezekiel (Ezek 1:3), Haggai (Hag 1:1), and Zechariah (Zech 1:1). On the other hand there is also an obvious connection with Luke 1:80, which affirms that John lived "in the deserts until the day of his manifestation before Israel."

Here John is not presented with the traditional name of "Baptist," but simply as the "son of Zechariah," something that the reader has already noted and which serves precisely to connect the new beginning with the preceding information. But why did this "son of Zechariah" grow up in the desert rather than in the Temple, which would have been more logical? Why did this son of a priest, whose birth was announced during the sacrifice of incense, show no interest in the cult of the Temple?

After the Qumran discovery there was no lack of scholars who interpreted John's permanence in the desert in terms of his affinity for the Essene movement. The hypothesis put forward was that John had spent part of his youth at Qumran, perhaps after the death of his elderly parents (who are not mentioned again in the Gospel). We know from Joseph Flavio (*The Jewish Wars*, 2, 8:2) that orphaned children, as well as those entrusted by their family to the care of the community, came to be educated at Qumran. This hypothesis, even if it cannot be proven, does not contradict the Lucan text.

Some scholars have advanced other arguments on the basis of John's spiritual proximity with the ambient of Qumran, in particular the element of water. They maintain that the importance attributed to ritual baths within the Qumran community may not be without connection to the baptism preached by John.

It seems to me that the text reveals a view opposed to that of the Qumran hypothesis. John, in fact, appears as a prophet called to prepare the coming of salvation not through study of the Law and ritual observance, as happened at Qumran, but through moral renewal, a courageous change of mentality and customs of which baptism in the Jordan would be the sign.

John's preaching manifests a strong eschatological character undoubtedly present also at Qumran, but, unlike the Teacher of righteousness (the leader of the Qumran community), the Baptist addresses himself to all the people and not to an elite group. Therefore, regarding the hypothesis that John had spent a certain period of time with the Essenes, one must conclude that at the time of his ministry he had already distanced himself from their positions.

Luke 3:3 describes John as an itinerant preacher ("he came to the whole region around the Jordan") in the manner of a herald, "proclaiming [*kerysson*] a baptism of repentance for the forgiveness of sins." The Baptist's mission is seen by Luke, and unanimously by all the other evangelists, as the fulfillment of the prophecy of Isaiah 40:3: John was the voice of one crying in the desert, who made "ready the way of the Lord." The return and the consolation of the people announced by the prophet are here interpreted in an ethical and eschatological sense.

The preaching of John

John is not simply a baptizer, as the name "Baptist" could mistakenly make us think; he is above all an evangelizer (cf. 3:18).

Luke depicts John as a preacher with a strong and direct style, who spoke without half measures and cut straight to the essentials. He called a thing by its true name, unmasking hypocrisies. Perhaps this is why John was so popular with the people.

John was not a pompous, arrogant preacher who spoke from on high to those beneath him and of whom it was not permitted to ask questions. Luke makes us see that the people questioned him. And the austere prophet of the desert had ears for everyone: for the crowd, but more particularly for the publicans—kept at a distance by the spiritual leaders of Judaism—and even for the soldiers.

In this way John preceded the Lord Jesus also in his manner of evangelizing. He is the precursor in his indiscriminate openness to all of Israel, since all Israel is called to conversion.

What does John say concretely? Before lingering over the details, let's take a comprehensive look at the literary composition of Luke 3:7–20. In it we find three points that illustrate many complementary aspects of the Baptist's preaching: the necessity to personally do good, without having recourse to the merits of Abraham (vv. 7–9); responsibly staying at our post in society (vv. 10–14); and, finally, witnessing to "him who will come" (vv. 15–20).

These three points are prefaced by clear stylistic elements:

1. "And to the crowds that were coming out to be baptized by him he said..." (v. 7);

2. "So the people questioned him and asked..." (v. 10);

3. "The people were in suspense.... John responded..." (v. 15f.).

In the first instance it is John who takes the initiative of speaking the word; in the second, the crowd, made up of certain categories of people, takes the initiative; and in the third it is again John who does so.

Worthy fruits of conversion

The first words placed in the mouth of John carry the cutting tone of the prophets of the Old Testament and run parallel to Matthew 11:7–19:

> "You brood of vipers! Who warned you to flee from the coming wrath? *Produce evidence* of your repentance, then, and don't go saying to yourselves, 'Abraham is our father!' for I say to you that God can raise up children to Abraham from these stones. Already now the axe is laid at the root of the trees; any tree, then, not *producing good fruit* will be cut down and thrown into the fire" (Lk 3:7–9).

Undoubtedly this was an unpleasant reprimand John directed to the people. In contrast with Matthew 3:7, which limits the invective to the Pharisees and the Sadducees, Luke extends it to all those who have come to be baptized.

Why are the children of Abraham equated with vipers? The image of snakes spitting deadly venom is certainly evocative: rather than being "a blessing for all the people," the children of Abraham have become deadly poisonous. The hard reproach is meant to provoke and elicit the call to conversion.

In effect, John is lashing out at empty presumption, the pride of belonging to a chosen people without living this people's spiritual heredity. Jesus will employ the same reproach in John 8:39: "If you're Abraham's children, do the *works* of Abraham!"

Useless flight

For the Baptist it is of no use "to escape into the desert" and rely on a rite of ablution that resembles those practiced at Qumran. Much less does it pay to escape into the past and count on the merits of the patriarchs. Conversion calls for personal responsibility to produce "fruits worthy of repentance." The baptism preached by John is not a rite that magically confers pardon of sins, but a "baptism of conversion" (cf. Lk 3:3); it is really this that obtains "the forgiveness of sins." Ethical duty is therefore placed decisively in the foreground and is sustained by eschatological motivations. John urges the people "to bear fruits worthy of conversion" because their days are numbered: "The axe is already laid to the root of the tree."

The apocalyptic flavor of this picture, to which the Baptist in fact refers in Luke 3:7, makes this idea of imminent judgment crystal clear. The barren tree is ready to be cut down to its roots, without any hope of deferment. Even the ancient prophets spoke of cutting down or a falling of trees (Isa 6:13; 10:33–34; 32:19). But closer similarities are found in Matthew, where Jesus himself, at the end of his first discourse, uses this image and the identical words: "Every tree not producing good fruit is cut down and thrown into the fire" (7:19). Likewise in John, the branches that did not bear fruit—says the Master—will be gathered and thrown into the fire and burned (see Jn 15:6).

Perceptible in the background is the thematic connection to what the angel had announced to the elderly Zechariah: "He will go before him...to make ready for the Lord a people made perfect" (Lk 1:17). This is typical of Luke's theology regarding the figure of the Baptist. Another noteworthy aspect is the attention John pays to the different social classes, particularly those who were marginalized in different ways by the leaders of Israel. Such attention is described in the second part of the passage (Lk 3:10–14), which is exclusive to Luke.

What should we do?

To John's warning—"Bear fruits worthy of repentance"—the question is put, "What are we to do [*ti poiesomen*]?" This question invariably resounds from the mouths of the crowd, of the publicans, and of the soldiers. It is also the question that the Church, significantly, hands down as the affirmation of conversion prior to receiving baptism (see Ac 2:37; 16:30).

John's answers comprise a rough outline of what could be called the social ethic of the New Testament. His first sentence underlines the necessity of sharing:

"Whoever has two tunics should share with the one who has none, and whoever has food should do likewise" (Lk 3:11).

This directive, addressed to the crowd, applies to everyone. It reinforces what is primary in the ethic of conversion. Conversion means re-establishing justice through the sharing of goods. The exhortation is not necessarily directed to the rich: to be personally challenged, it is enough that one has two coats. The Baptist's aim is not to praise poverty, as if having one tunic were the ideal. His point is to share. It is charity, fraternal love for one who has no other coat, that can obtain for us divine mercy and "the forgiveness of sins."

What comes to mind here is Jesus' radical proposal to his itinerant disciples not to have two tunics (see Lk 9:3). In that situation the invitation is dictated by the faith the missionaries must have in Providence. But as expressed by John, the sharing of goods is in fact strictly connected to the idea of covenant, together with the ideal of equality and the confidence in divine care that it brings with it.

In a certain sense this general directive interprets and updates the commandment, "You shall love your neighbor as yourself." John's responses to the tax collectors and soldiers apply the same commandment in the concrete and diverse situations of life.

Although the tax collectors' line of work ends up on the rabbinical list of shameful and infamous types of occupation, John does not ask them to give up their profession. He holds that even tax collectors can have a sincere desire for conversion; that conversion can happen effectively within every social class. This is why John does not refuse baptism to tax collectors. He responds to their question in terms of professional ethics: "Collect nothing more than what has been designated for you" (Lk 3:13). Likewise soldiers are required not to maltreat others and to be content with their wages.

One is coming who is more powerful than I

The background against which the preaching of the Baptist is set is one filled with strong eschatological expectation. The people live in almost agonizing expectation, and come to question whether John himself might not be the Messiah. In a way, John has fueled people's anxiety with his preaching of imminent judgment. Still, he does not feed any false understanding that may exist in people's minds, and is concerned about clarifying, from the start, ambiguities regarding the right identity of the Messiah. He says openly:

> "I baptize you with water, but one more powerful than I is coming, the strap of whose sandal I am not worthy to untie; he will baptize you with the Holy Spirit and fire—his winnowing shovel is in his hand to clean out his threshing floor and gather his grain into the barn, but he will burn the chaff with unquenchable fire" (Lk 3:16–17).

Placed in the mouth of the precursor, these words are a taste of prophetic Christology; they are almost the "inheritance" that the Baptist picked up from the "Law and the Prophets" (Lk 16:16) about the mission of the long-expected One. The words are nearly identical to those found in Matthew 3:11–12 and also, in part, in Mark 1:7–8 and John 1:27.

The Messiah is described with expressions that show clearly his superiority to the Baptist: he is "more powerful," he baptizes not simply with water, but with the Spirit and fire. Post-exilic Judaism waited with great longing for the eschatological communication of the Spirit. The actual realization of this lively expectation is described by Luke in the Pentecost event (Ac 1:5; 2:33), in the pouring out of the Holy Spirit even on the Gentiles, as happened in the house of Cornelius (Ac 10:44; 11:15).

He who will baptize with the Holy Spirit and fire is also really the eschatological Judge and the Lord of the harvest. John, who has appealed to people to bear fruits worthy of repentance, concludes by confirming that it is not he, but One who is stronger, who is able to pick out good fruit from the dross; in other words, to give definitive judgment. And so, in Luke, the preaching of the Baptist starts from ethics, passes on to a kerygmatic announcement of the One who is to come after him, and ends by showing that this is the very One who will weigh the fruit worthy of conversion. The fruit that John asks for will then be welcomed by the Messiah and, freed from the dross, will be introduced once and for all into the Kingdom. It is the Messiah who is the Lord of the harvest; John is not worthy even to be his slave, the servant who unties the thong of his sandals.

Luke concludes with a finishing touch all his own, applying to the preaching of the Baptist the verb "to evangelize," which later will distinguish the activity of Jesus and his disciples: "With many other exhortations he *evangelized* the people" (see 3:18).

John did not preach the Kingdom of God in itself. He preached about the One who was to come and testified that it would be he who judged. John's ethical preaching, introduced with strong eschatological motivations (the axe laid to the root of the tree), takes on a definitive Christological conclusion. He establishes an ethic of conversion potentially Christological. Therefore, even his vehement call to penitence constitutes Good News, a message of salvation.

CHAPTER 5

Jesus of Nazareth is sent
to evangelize the poor

*L*uke does not describe the baptism of Jesus. Unlike
Mark and Matthew, his attention is not focused on
the Nazarene descending into the Jordan. Instead, he concentrates on the descent of the Spirit upon Jesus, almost as
if to point out the immediate fulfillment of John's words:
The "one who is more powerful," he who will baptize in
the Holy Spirit and fire, is the first himself to be baptized
in the Spirit.

Declared the chosen Son of the Father, Jesus is the man
whom God has dreamed of, the descendant who ennobles
the progenitor of the human family, the new Adam full of
the Holy Spirit. This is the meaning of Luke's genealogy,
placed immediately after the outpouring of the Spirit (Lk
3:23–38).

All of Jesus' activity, his prophetic and healing ministry,
manifests itself in light of this baptismal event. The Jesus

whom Luke portrays is moved, conducted, held, and taken back not by his own independent decision, but by the power of the Spirit. Twice within the same verse Luke underlines the presence and the movement of the Spirit in Jesus' life: "Jesus returned from the Jordan full of the Holy Spirit and was led by the Spirit through the desert" (Lk 4:1).

Jesus consecrated by the Spirit

Jesus' public life is shown in full docility to the Spirit who leads him. Luke sees the life of the Church in the same light: it is not simply Peter and the apostles who decide what needs to be done, but "the Holy Spirit and we" who decide (Ac 15:28); it is not really Paul and his companions who decide where to evangelize, but the Spirit of Jesus, who may not be in agreement with the projected destination (cf. Ac 16:7).

Following Jesus' baptism in the Jordan the Spirit leads him into the desert, the place of prayer, of fasting, and of battle with evil. "After [Satan] had exhausted every temptation" (cf. Lk 4:13)—that is, after forty days—the devil leaves him to return later, at another opportune time (i.e., the passion); and in the power of the Spirit, Jesus returns to Galilee. His fame spreads rapidly. There is not a place that does not speak about him: "And he taught in their synagogues, praised by all" (Lk 4:15).

On his visit to Nazareth, his home town, he is preceded by his fame as a healer. Luke purposely chooses the synagogue—frequented by Jesus from the time he was a child—

and the liturgical service of the Sabbath for the announcement of Jesus' program of evangelization.

From the outset there is great rejoicing in the synagogue of Nazareth. But it takes little for this joy to transform itself into anger and even murderous rage. Why is Jesus not able to accomplish even one miracle in his own town? Why does he have to go elsewhere to bring the Good News?

Jesus, the evangelizer in the power of the Spirit, begins his ministry with failure. From the third Gospel's point of view, the mystery of the cross is already taking shape.

In the synagogue of Nazareth

Two opposing scenes

Luke 4:16–30 can easily be articulated in two parts, characterized respectively by the "coming" (4:16–22) and by the dramatic "going" of Jesus (4:23–30). "He came," *elthen,* is the first word of the passage; the last is "he went on his way," *eporeueto.*

The coming of Jesus to Nazareth takes place in a climate of strong expectation, reaching its peak in the wonder and amazement of the crowds gathered there. But between verses 22 and 23 there is an abrupt change of tone, noted by Scripture commentators. From an atmosphere of welcome we pass very quickly to revolt. Jesus' provocative stance in this discourse culminates in his rejection by the Nazarenes and their dramatic attempt to kill him (4:23–30).

The entire scene is put together with great accuracy and reveals Luke's careful hand. Verses 16–20 show a well-balanced arrangement, at the center of which we find the text from Isaiah.

> *A.*   ...As was his custom he went into the SYNAGOGUE...
>   and **he stood up** to read.
>   *They handed him the scroll* of the prophet Isaiah,
>   and when he unrolled the scroll he found
>   the place where it was written...
>
>   **B.**   [Citation of Isa 61 and 58]
>
> *AA.*   When he had rolled up the scroll
>   and *handed it back to the attendant*
>   **he sat down,**
>   and the eyes of everyone in the SYNAGOGUE
>   were fixed on him.

The first scene

From the time he was a boy Jesus frequented the synagogue of Nazareth, where everyone knew him and had witnessed him grow up and become a man. Significantly, Luke places the "revelation" of Jesus' mission in the context of the liturgy of Saturday morning, when the entire population is there, gathered for worship.

One supposes that the reading from the Torah (the Pentateuch) has already taken place, as well as the prayers making up the first part of the rite: the "eighteen blessings," the profession of faith, and the blessing of the priest (Num 11:24ff.).

And he got up to read

Jesus gets up to do the second reading, taken from the prophets. One notes that Jesus' proper name is missing in this passage. This can be ascribed to "typical Lucan economy."[1] Such an omission reinforces the connection with the "true beginning" described in the preceding summary (4:14–15): "Jesus returned to Galilee in the power of the Spirit" (4:14a). In verse 16, Luke does not feel the need to repeat Jesus' name; not mentioning it reinforces the centrality of the protagonist.

What is emphasized above all in this passage is Jesus' initiative. He freely gets up to take on the task of reading in public (nothing is said of a possible invitation on the part of the president of the synagogue, although it would be logical to assume that such was extended).

The narrative goes straight to the point. In the scroll of Isaiah, Jesus finds the text that serves to reveal the character of the promise contained in the Scriptures and their present fulfillment. He refers here to the passage of Isaiah 61:1–2a.

But the text actually cited by Luke 4:18–19 combines two passages from Isaiah, and it is unthinkable that Jesus would have found it written this way in the scroll he was given at Nazareth. After he reads the citation of Isaiah 61:1, Jesus goes on to Isaiah 58:6, then returns to Isaiah 61:2, which is, however, interrupted first by the second half of the verse, omitting any reference to the "day of vengeance" (Isa

---

1. J.-N. Aletti, *L'arte di raccontare Gesù Cristo* (Brescia: 1991), 40.

61:2b; the citation by Luke follows the Greek text of the Septuagint).

The last line of Luke 4:18, missing in Isaiah 61—"to let the oppressed go free"—is taken up by Isaiah 58:6 and shows the year of grace as a year of "liberation."

Taken as a whole, this citation serves to interpret the event of Jesus' baptism (Lk 3:21ff.). Through the text from Isaiah, we are being told that the Spirit's descent and resting on Jesus at the Jordan really signifies the messianic anointing. Jesus is consecrated by the Spirit to evangelize the poor.

And the eyes of all in the synagogue were fixed on him

An air of great *suspense* hangs over the synagogue. The eyes of all present are fixed on Jesus, ready to take in his every movement, his every word. But Jesus does not give the traditional "homily." Words of "explanation" do not come from his mouth; rather, he issues a solemn "declaration." He proclaims the fulfillment of the prophecy just read: *"Today this Scripture has been fulfilled in your hearing"* (Lk 4:21).

We notice the echo of Mark's cry: *"The time is fulfilled"* (Mk 1:15). But here, even more than in Mark, we have the fulfillment of this expectation with and in Jesus: "The Spirit of the Lord [rests] upon me" (Lk 4:18).

The fulfillment is realized "today" (*semeron*). It is the salvific "today" that is revealed to the oppressed and to sinners, the today that resounds also for the thief crucified with Jesus: "This day you will be with me in paradise" (Lk 23:43).

"Today this Scripture has been fulfilled *in your hearing*" (Lk 4:21).

Here one notes an exchange in the position of the "eyes" with the "ears." Those present want *to see* ("the eyes of all"), but Jesus takes them back to the biblical pre-eminence of *listening* to the Word, in which hearing—and not sight—enables understanding of the accomplishment of the promise. Its fulfillment, in fact, is discovered in the revealing *power* (*dynamis)* of the Word.

The Scriptures are fulfilled here and now, in this time and place; not merely in the "synagogue," but more specifically through personal listening: "in your hearing."

And all spoke well of him....

At first the self-revelation of Jesus is favorably accepted at Nazareth. The words that come from his mouth are judged by his fellow townspeople as "gracious words" (*logoi tes charitos*), words revealing the grace that saves. In this sense the Nazarenes echo what has already been said of him throughout the whole region, full of his renown (Lk 4:14), and in the various synagogues of Galilee where all are praising him (Lk 4:15).

But at Nazareth there is a particular element not found elsewhere: here the people have seen Jesus grow up under their own eyes; they not only know him but believe they know everything about him: Is he not the son of Joseph? (v. 22b)

Here at Nazareth praise is mixed with the kind of amazement that comes very close to the question the evangelist John places in the mouth of the Jews: "Where did the fellow get this learning, since he has not studied?" (Jn 7:15)

The second scene

In the second part, the passage changes tone and dramatically anticipates the story of the passion. The change is introduced by an intervention of Jesus, who intends to interpret the feelings of those present.

The proverb he cites ("Physician, heal thyself," v. 23) makes it clear that the Nazarenes are waiting for "deeds" and not just beautiful words, for prodigies similar to those that took place in Capernaum. But Jesus, quoting another saying—"No prophet is acceptable in his hometown"— makes it understood that at Nazareth he will not perform any miracles.

The language of these verses is strongly allusive. There is a subtle play at unmasking the sentiments and intentions of his audience—indirectly—by referring to the stories of the prophets, specifically of Elijah and Elisha.

At the end of verses 25–27, Jesus speaks of the preaching of salvation to the pagans. He too is destined to work in a "foreign" country (at Capernaum), and one day salvation will go not to Israel, who refused it, but to the Gentiles (see Ac 13:46; 28:28).

The widow of Zarephath

With delicate artistry, Luke depicts in the widow of Zarephath the conditions that allow Jesus to work miracles and to heal:

"But I tell you in truth, there were many widows in Israel in the days of Elijah, when the sky was shut up for three years and six months while there was a severe famine over all the land, yet Elijah was sent to none of them except to Zarephath of Sidon, to a woman, a widow. And there were many lepers in Israel in the time of Elisha the prophet, yet none of them was cleansed except Naaman the Syrian" (Lk 4:25–27).

In the already overheated synagogue of Nazareth, Jesus recalls the memory of a woman and man who were foreigners yet who benefited from the mercy of God. But what in particular did the widow of Zarephath have that placed her above the many widows living in Israel at the time of the prophet Elijah?

First of all, this is about a "widow." Luke is especially attentive to the so-called weaker classes—women, the marginalized, and children. Without a doubt among these classes, "widows" are in the forefront in terms of vulnerability. This was not so much because of their physical weakness as the difficulties that a single woman faced in order to receive justice, to make her voice and her rights heard in the world of the powerful. A widow no longer had a husband to defend and protect her.

In the story mentioned by Jesus, we are dealing with a very poor widow. First Kings 17:9–24 vividly describes this woman's situation of poverty. Elijah encounters her at the city gate and appeals to her because he is thirsty: "Bring me a little water...so that I may drink" (v. 10).

This scene takes place in the middle of a drought, in which a "little water" is a precious commodity. But Elijah immediately adds still another request: "As she was going to bring it, he called to her and said, 'Bring me a morsel of bread...'" (v. 11).

At this point the text fully reveals the desperate conditions in which the woman is trying to live:

> "As the LORD your God lives, I have nothing baked, only a handful of meal in a jar, and a little oil in a jug; I am now gathering a couple of sticks, so that I may go home and prepare it for myself and my son, that we may eat it, and die" (1 Kings 17:12).

The woman's situation is dire; nonetheless, the prophet insists:

> "Do not be afraid; go and do as you have said; but first make me a little cake of it and bring it to me, and afterwards make something for yourself and your son. For thus says the LORD the God of Israel: The jar of meal will not be emptied and the jug of oil will not fail until the day that the LORD sends rain on the earth" (1 Kings 17:13–14).

We have the advantage of knowing that Elijah is a great prophet, but the woman did not yet know this; still "she went and did as Elijah said" just the same. This, then, is the widow of Zarephath! She is a woman who has faith in the Word of God and who puts herself at great risk even though she does not yet know Elijah as a prophet. She is not a simpleton. She is a woman who has the courage to risk herself and her own survival.

Generally those who truly dare to risk are not the rich, but the poor. In her poverty, the widow of Zarephath welcomes the stranger and shares with him her last piece of bread. What was at stake for her was her and her son's last day of life. And Jesus holds her up as an example of true faith, faith he did not find in his fellow countrymen. The widow of Zarephath represents the person who has a faith capable of risking. This is the faith that can somehow call forth the healing energy of Jesus, prompting him to say: "Your faith has saved you!"

And he went on his way...

Jesus' remarks in the synagogue of Nazareth conclude with the revolt of the townspeople and their unsuccessful attempt to kill him (see Lk 4:29–30).

In this scene the last sentence contains a verb that is dear to the Christology of Luke: "And he went away."

Where did he go? Toward the mission for which the Spirit had consecrated him—first to Capernaum, then to all of Galilee and neighboring regions, and finally to Jerusalem, since no prophet can die except in Jerusalem (see Lk 13:13). But not even death stops Jesus, for the Gospel of Luke concludes with his journey to heaven.

If no one at Nazareth benefited from the healing action of Jesus due to their lack of faith, in other places people experience the same benefits as the widow of Zarephath and Naaman the Syrian.

After the rejection of his fellow Nazarenes, Jesus' immediate goal is Capernaum, on the northeast shore of the Lake of Galilee. Here Luke takes up Mark's narrative thread, the so-called "day in Capernaum."

It is during the Sabbath—therefore, at least a week after what happened in Nazareth—and the key moments of the day are recounted almost in slow motion: in the morning, the liturgical service in the synagogue; at noon, the festive meal in the house of Simon; after sunset, at the end of the Sabbath, the healing of the many who are sick (4:33–41). What takes place on this first day is highly significant. Jesus puts both man and woman back on their feet, together restored with their specific roles.

In the end, the healing and liberating activity of the Lord is extended to all the needy, and on each one "he laid his hands" (4:40). This last element, exclusive to Luke, underlines the restoration that Jesus intends to offer to each person, man and woman; an action that recovers one's original image and rescues one from the power of evil, an action that enables praise and service.

At Nazareth Jesus was presented as the prophet consecrated "to bring the Good News to the poor...to proclaim release to captives and recovery of sight to the blind, to set at liberty the oppressed" (4:18). It is a vision that unfolds one step at a time as the Gospel moves forward.

Jesus' mission of evangelization does not "obey" people's expectations, even those of his relatives or fellow townspeople; it does not allow itself to be rushed by a false sense of urgency. Rather, it docilely entrusts itself to the movement of the Spirit, perceived in prayer.

CHAPTER 6

Men and women along the way of the Gospel

*T*hroughout chapter 4 of the Gospel, Jesus acts alone; Luke does not even name the disciples until chapter 5. It's almost as if at the beginning of the Gospel he wants to focus his attention only on Jesus. This is highly significant, inasmuch as with this approach Luke distinctly veers away from the outlook Mark takes. It is said that Mark does not know how to imagine Jesus' activity apart from that of his disciples. In fact, the opening announcement of the Kingdom in Mark's Gospel is followed immediately by the call of the first four disciples (see Mk 1:14–20); they enter Capernaum together, then proceed to the synagogue and to the house of Simon (see Mk 1:21–29). When Jesus leaves the house very early the next morning, retiring to a solitary place to pray, it is Simon and those of his household who, feeling responsible for their guest, go to look for Jesus (see Mk 1:35–37).

Not so in Luke. Jesus enters Simon's house before Simon is even a disciple. In the morning, when the Master draws apart for prayer, it is the crowd that looks for him, not Simon. This point demonstrates the freedom of the Lord and the breadth of his mission. He cannot tie himself down to one house, nor even to Capernaum; he must preach the Good News of the Kingdom of God also in other cities and teach in other synagogues (see Lk 4:43).

Chapter 4 closes with the image of Jesus, the itinerant preacher who is still on his own. As already mentioned, the call of the first disciples takes place in chapter 5. On one hand, Luke seems to be familiar with Mark's account, which presents the call of Simon and his companions according to a script borrowed straight from the Old Testament, in the classic manner of vocation stories: he passed, he saw, he called, and they left everything and followed him (see Mk 1:16–20). On the other hand, Luke does not rigidly hold himself to this format, which perhaps he considers too dry and detached. Instead, he assimilates everything into a story that is much more personal and full of emotion.

Simon and his companions

The call of Simon cuts through the whole of daily life, with its fears and contradictions.

We find ourselves situated, as in Mark and Matthew, along the shore of the lake. A sizable crowd is present, a sign of the success Jesus' preaching is starting to enjoy.

People are gathering around him "in order to hear the Word of God" (Lk 5:1). Jesus, standing on the coast of Gennesaret, spots two empty boats still on the shore. The fishermen have disembarked and are washing their nets.

It is not mentioned whether Simon has been listening to Jesus or not. From the context, however, it seems he is rather absorbed in his work. Jesus is the one who takes the initiative and climbs into Simon's boat. Although the text doesn't say so directly, it is easy to imagine that, seeing Jesus get into his boat, Simon would quickly shift his gaze from the nets and direct them obligingly toward the Master, who seems to be showing a special interest in him.

Jesus had already come to his house as a guest, and now he is getting into Simon's boat, preferring his to all the others that are moored along the shore, most likely those of the sons of Zebedee, his partners. Simon therefore removes his focus from the nets and directs his attention to the Master, who is honoring him with special preference. Jesus, returning his gaze, asks him to pull out a short distance from the shore, after which he sits down and teaches the crowds from the boat (5:3).

When his preaching is finished, Jesus tells Simon to put out to sea and lower the nets for a catch. The figure of the Church is easily discernible in this image: The boat in which the Master instructs, as from a teacher's chair (the verb used is *kathizo,* from which the term *cathedra* is derived), must put out to sea and gather an immense quantity of fish.

The great catch of fish

So begins the compelling story of Simon's vocation. These few remarks are enough to testify to the personal way in which Luke means to recount this event.

It is late in the day and Simon, an experienced fisherman, puts forward his objections. The young Master explains the Word of God with unquestionable competence, but when it comes to fishing he seems to understand little or nothing. It is not his fault; he is from Nazareth, from the hills, and he has no experience of the sea. Simon protests, therefore: "We've been at it all night [the ideal time for fishing], working hard, and have caught nothing, but at your word I will lower the nets" (Lk 5:5).

Once again it is worth pointing out our evangelist's unique viewpoint. In fact, it is not by chance that these are the first words that Luke puts in Simon's mouth. Not so in the Gospel of Mark, where Peter already intervenes in chapter 1, when he finds the Master absorbed in prayer and, perhaps wondering why his guest left the house without saying anything, makes himself the spokesman of the collective search party: "Everyone is looking for you!" (Mk 1:37) Luke, in the parallel passage (4:42–43), omits this remark. He reserves Peter's first words for the occasion of his call.

These words are totally Simon, and very true to life. They express his good sense, his clear understanding and professional ability on the one hand, and, on the other, his complete and unconditional trust in the Master, which will characterize him. Perhaps another person would have laughed and commented with some irony that the young Rabbi understood nothing of the rules of fishing. Why would anyone attempt to fish in such adverse conditions, when even in the most favorable of times, during the night, they labored for nothing?

Simon shows his confusion and points out to the Master the objective difficulty in the undertaking. But he does not use this difficulty as an excuse. He is sincerely ready to trust Jesus. *You ask me to do this, and that is enough for me to let down the nets.*

Simon's first words have already crossed over to a logic of love, one characterized by unconditional trust. "When they did this," continues the text—that is, when they lowered their nets—"they took in a tremendous number of fish, but their nets began to rip" (5:6). It was even necessary to call for help to their partners, who were following in another boat. And they filled both boats, almost to the point of sinking.

This experience of fishing—going against good sense and the dictates of the trade, but manifesting extraordinary results nonetheless—has a strong impact on Simon. Overcome by awe, he falls to his knees before Jesus, exclaiming:

"Leave me, Lord, for I am a sinful man!" (5:8)

In saying, "Go away from me" (literally: get out, go far away from me), perhaps Peter means to ask Jesus to leave his house, his family. By coming into Simon's home, Jesus became like family. But now his person is revealed to Peter in a new and rather frightening light: as an extraordinary person, one who is certainly a man of God!

Luke notes that such amazement has gripped not only Simon and those who were with him, but also his partners in the other boat, James and John, the sons of Zebedee, who have helped Simon bring all of those fish to shore.

Fishers of men

From these extraordinary events and from their resulting emotional impact, Jesus draws a conclusion that is diametrically opposed to that of Simon. Instead of "going far away" from him, as Simon has asked, Jesus reassures the distraught fisherman and calls him decidedly to himself, associating Simon with his mission of salvation:

"Don't be afraid; from now on you will be catching men" (5:10).

Jesus will not leave Simon's house or family; instead, he calls the members of this family to himself and transforms their livelihood. And immediately Simon and his companions "brought their boats to land...left everything and followed him" (5:11), as though his call cast over them an irresistible fascination.

Jesus had proven himself: he showed that he knew how to direct extraordinary fishing on the lake. Why not trust him also when there is a possibility of a new kind of adventure, that of fishing for men? Perhaps without fully understanding, Simon and his companions entrust themselves to the word of Jesus, to the point that everything else becomes secondary to them. By now, all that counts is to follow Jesus.

We find in this narration something similar to what we read at the conclusion of the Gospel of John, in the miraculous catch of fish at the third manifestation of the Risen One. There the fishing is followed with breakfast on the shore of the lake and with the triple question of love that Jesus asks of Simon Peter (see Jn 21:1–19). Here we're dealing with a new beginning; with the restoration of Simon, after his denial on the night of Jesus' betrayal, to the role of leader and guide. What better way than to place the new beginning on the shore of that lake that had witnessed the generous response of the apostle and his courage to leave everything for the Kingdom of God?

In both scenes Jesus is the one who takes the initiative, not abandoning his disciple when he feels lost. Simon is in fact distressed when Jesus, for the third time, asks him about the truth of his love for him: "Peter was distressed because he had said to him a third time, 'Do you love me?' And he said to him, 'Lord, you know everything; you know that I love you!'" (Jn 21:17) Certainly the memory of his words that first day come back to him: "Leave me, Lord, for I am a sinful man!" (Lk 5:8) But on both occasions, Jesus does not go away. On the contrary, he associates Peter's work with his own: "From now on you will be catching men" (Lk 5:10); "Tend my sheep!" (Jn 21:17)

Levi, the tax collector

In the call of the first disciples Jesus shows how true was the program he outlined at Nazareth: that he was called to evangelize the poor and to free the oppressed. The call of Levi, the tax collector, demonstrates to the maximum his desire to save. The Master calls both one who feels himself to be a sinner (Peter) and one who is considered so by others (Levi).

In recounting the vocation of Levi, Luke puts forward explicitly and for the first time the imperative to follow. "Follow me" is the message Jesus directs to Levi, seated at his tax booth (Lk 5:27).

The answer is immediate, just like that of the disciples who were first called, but that is all. Levi celebrates the event with a great banquet to which he invites his publican friends. As the evangelist points out, a "large number" is present. Without a doubt, Levi was a man of importance in his hometown, and his vocation would have been the cause of much talk in Capernaum and the surrounding area.

Perhaps Simon, on his part, begins to understand the meaning of Jesus' words: "You will be fishing for men." Levi is certainly a big fish!

Discussions at table

That banquet is not without tension. Some who are present are scandalized and even indignant: "Why do you eat and drink with tax collectors and sinners?" This is the question that the Pharisees and scribes ask the disciples of Jesus (Lk 5:30).

The response comes directly from the Master: "Those in good health are not in need of a doctor—the sick are; I have come to call not the righteous, but sinners to repentance" (5:31–32).

A solemn conclusion, which confirms the program announced in the synagogue at Nazareth. A conclusion which is deliberately provocative. Those with a keen interest in the Law would have to ask themselves the "why" of this drawing near to tax collectors and sinners. What reasons pushed Jesus to call those who were far away and to eat and celebrate with them? What reasons other than the unconditional offer of salvation and the proclamation of a year of favor from the Lord (cf. Lk 4:19)?

An itinerant group

And now Jesus becomes more systematic in his evangelization of Israel; it becomes a kind of "blanket evangelization": "He went traveling through city and village..." (Lk 8:1).

Luke presents an interesting development in the activity of Jesus. After the call of the first disciples, and in particular after the conversion of Levi, the group of disciples seems already to be a considerable number. In fact, shortly after, Jesus will be able to choose from among them "twelve apostles." Together with him they will form a permanent group.

But there were not just these twelve men. Luke is the only evangelist who from the beginning of Jesus' ministry records the presence of women. They were the ones who followed the Master to his death, without betraying him and without running away on that important night. They were with him from the start in Galilee, completely understanding his goal and purpose, and fully sharing their goods with him.

Luke bears witness to a feminine discipleship from the initial moments of Jesus' preaching in Galilee. Unlike the rabbis of his time, Jesus holds that women too can and must listen and understand the Word of God. He challenges the dominant culture not only because he allows himself to be touched by women who were sinners, but much more because he considers women capable of theology (in this regard, besides the account of Luke 10:38–42, there is also the wonderful episode in John with the dialogue between Jesus and the Samaritan woman, which touches on points of true theological debate: see Jn 4:7–26).

Whether dealing with masculine or feminine vocations, Jesus is the one who clarifies the precise method of following him. It is not up to a man or a woman to choose the "how." One remembers the Master's response to the former Gerasene demoniac, who had asked to follow Jesus permanently. Jesus did not permit him to, but told him: "Go off to your home, to your own people, and proclaim to them everything the Lord has done for you and how he had mercy on you" (Mk 5:19). Analogously, Jesus decides the form, whether itinerant or resident, of feminine discipleship. He accepts that some women will follow him and his disciples in their travels, and that others will welcome them into their own homes.

The itinerant women disciples

The news of a feminine itinerant group is given in a "summary" that is meant to inform the Gospel reader about the evangelizing activity of Jesus:

> It happened next that he went traveling through city and village, preaching and proclaiming the Good News of the Kingdom of God, and the twelve were with him as well as some women who had been healed from evil spirits and illnesses—Mary, who was called the Magdalen, from whom seven demons had gone out, and Joanna, the wife of Chuza, Herod's steward, and Susanna, and many others who provided for them out of their possessions (Lk 8:1–3).

What role do these women play? First of all, their mention in Jesus' group of itinerant disciples is important. In fact, it constitutes an absolute novelty in the culture of the time, particularly in the environment of Palestine.

The text tells us that these women have experienced the exorcising and healing power of Jesus—they "had been healed from evil spirits and illnesses"—and that "they provided [*diekonoun*] for them out of their possessions."

Their ministry included the various needs of an itinerant group—women made capable of energetic and active love by the grace they had received, just like the forgiven woman (cf. Lk 7:36–50).

Mary Magdalen

Mary Magdalen occupies first place in the list mentioned in Luke 8; she is a leader known by all four of the evangelists in their account of the resurrection. Undoubtedly she was an outstanding woman in the early Christian community.

Before following Jesus, Mary was exorcized "of seven demons." Possession by seven spirits is a particularly serious case according to Luke 11:26. Is it then correct to interpret these "seven demons" in a sexual way and to see in the Magdalen the "sinner" (prostitute) of whom the account immediately preceding this one speaks?

From antiquity the image of the forgiven woman, whose name Luke does not mention, has been superimposed on Mary of Magdala, from whom "seven devils had gone out" (see Lk 7:37–50). To have seven devils is interpreted as having the devil of all devils, the sexual demon, the devilry that is expressed in sex, *porneia*. From this comes the traditional image of Magdalen the former prostitute, who lets down her long hair to dry the tears that have fallen on Jesus' feet.

From Luke's summary, Mary of Magdala emerges as a woman restored to herself, freed from demonic power and given back her liberty. And this woman, restored to herself, now lives her freedom in the service of love (cf. Gal 5:1–15).

Joanna

The second woman mentioned in Luke 8:3 is Joanna. There is no reference to her in the other two synoptic accounts or in John. Luke, instead, mentions her both here and later in 24:10, where her name again appears immediately after that of Mary of Magdala.

Joanna is the wife of Chuza, Herod's steward. She therefore comes from a situation of social privilege. But how is it that, being married, she belongs to a group of itinerant disciples following Jesus? Luke doesn't explain.

Was she perhaps a widow? If that were the case, it is curious that Luke did not say so, since he showed consistent admiration for Christian widows. The text also seems to rule out the idea that Joanna had been abandoned by her husband, since she is presented as his "wife." Joanna's situation, then, appears all the more complex. Was Chuza in agreement with her choice to follow Jesus? And if not, did she have to put up with hostility and the loss of her husband's affection? Nothing is said of the possible presence of children.

But, beyond all this, what could have been the reason that compelled this woman to follow Jesus? Luke does not even answer this question explicitly. We could suppose that what was said of the other women might apply equally to her; that she also had somehow experienced healing and liberation.

Susanna

The third woman mentioned in Luke 8:3 is Susanna, of whom we know nothing other than her name. However, it is enough to conclude that a concrete group of women traveled with Jesus and the other disciples, and their names were still remembered by the early Christian community at the time the Gospel of Luke was written. The same good fortune was not had by the woman who, on the eve of the passion, anointed Jesus' head with expensive perfume worth 300 denarii (see Mk 14:3–9).

These women had the courage to live outside of traditional values; the strength to face and overcome difficulties and privations inherent in following Jesus and his untiring itinerary.

The disciples who stayed at home

Luke also tells of other female disciples who did not accompany the Master on his journeys, but who were offered as models of welcome and hospitality. They were women who opened their home to the Lord Jesus, served him, and listened to his word.

The house of Martha

The story of Martha and Mary (see Lk 10:38–42) is placed within the context of mission. Chapter 10 opens with the sending out of the seventy-two disciples, and the information given at the beginning of the story is that Jesus and his group were on "the course of their journey" (v. 38).

In the fatigue and burden of the mission they find generous hospitality with two sisters. Martha is introduced first; most likely she is the older of the two and owner of the house, since it is expressly called "hers." Furthermore, Mary is introduced in relation to Martha: "She had a sister named Mary" (v. 39).

The two sisters relate to Jesus in very different ways. Martha is concerned with offering him a beautiful welcome, which includes performing "many tasks." Mary, instead, "seated herself at the Lord's feet and listened to his teaching."

What we have here is most likely an idiomatic expression. "To stay at the feet of" someone means to be a disciple of that person. One thinks of St. Paul, who said of himself: "I grew up at the feet of Gamaliel," an obvious reference to his rabbinical formation. Gamaliel was one of the most famous rabbis of Paul's time.

In such a situation, Mary, by her attitude, is violating the role of women established by the Judaic culture of the time, which determined that women's place was in the kitchen and men's was at the study of Scripture.

Mary's part

Martha does not look upon her sister's transgression in a very favorable light, and she marvels that the Master does not take a stand. She frankly tells him how things are, shares with him her point of view, and asks for support: "Lord, doesn't it matter to you that my sister has left me to serve alone?" (v. 40) *It should matter to you, since you care about everyone; well, in this case, the injured party is me:* "Tell her to give me a hand."

In this manner, Martha asks Jesus for help in bringing her sister back within the acceptable parameters of a woman's given role. But Jesus will have none of it. He sides with Mary who, in her apparent non-activity, has dared to transgress prevailing norms.

This "sitting at Jesus' feet" as a male disciple would do coincides with the choice of the "better part, which will not be taken from her" (v. 42), because Jesus has no intention of taking this right away from her. Mary—and with her, all women who desire it—may remain at the feet of Jesus, as do the male disciples.

In conclusion, Martha's house cannot limit itself to being a place of refreshment. By the fact that the Master is present, it becomes a place of evangelization, a place of the Word, *Bet hammidrash*, that is, "a house of study and interpretation of Scripture," open not only to men but to women as well.

CHAPTER 7

Jesus rejoices for the things that are revealed to little ones

*I*n the preceding reflections we have observed how the Good News brought about blessings and inspired song right from the beginning of the Gospel of Luke, involving people of both sexes who were humble and simple. In this *lectio* we want to pause over Jesus' prayer in conjunction with the return of the seventy-two whom he had sent out to evangelize.

With good reason Luke is being hailed more and more as the "evangelist of prayer." In fact, he above all others portrays Jesus in prayer and implies the importance of this for the evangelizing mission of the Church. It is enough to take a quick look at the numbers. The verb to pray (*proseuchesthai*) recurs fifteen times in Matthew, ten times in Mark, thirty-five times in Luke/Acts, and never in John, who prefers to express the idea of prayer with the verb to ask (*erotao*). Analogously, the noun for prayer (*proseuchê*) crops up twice in Matthew, twice again in Mark, and twelve times in Luke/Acts. Moreover, Luke makes use of a wide range of terms to indicate "prayer," such as to praise (*ainein*), to bless (*eulogein*), to glorify (*doxazein*), to give thanks (*eucharistein*), and to pray (*deisthai/deêsis*).

The theme of Jesus at prayer is a fascinating one, but it is also difficult and demanding. We are dealing with the singular relationship that unites Jesus with his Father, a relationship of incredible filial intimacy. Jesus' always being there for others; his bending low, full of mercy and compassion for the sufferings and sicknesses that afflict people; his untiring preaching of the Kingdom of God— all pours forth from this vital center and constantly returns to it. Jesus makes no decisions, especially if they are important ones, without first having prayed. Prayer runs through his life as a reality into which everything is wrapped and by which everything is penetrated.

Father, into your hands

Jesus lives in constant dialogue with the Father, turning to him to understand his will and accomplish it perfectly. From this comes the nights spent in prayer, as well as the Master's spontaneous explosion of praise and blessing (cf. Lk 10:21–22). And from this prayer comes that supreme handing over of himself to the Father in unlimited trust at the moment of his trial and death.

Jesus begins his mission in prayer, in the presence of God. This aspect was already introduced in the account of the baptism. Unlike Mark and Matthew, Luke does not mention that Jesus went down and came up from the waters of the Jordan; he focuses directly on the fact that Jesus "was in prayer" (Lk 3:21). It is during prayer that the heavens are opened and the Holy Spirit descends and comes to rest on Jesus in corporeal form, while the voice of the Father reveals him as the "beloved son" (Lk 3:22).

It is the same on the mount of the Transfiguration. Luke is the only one to point out that Jesus went up the mountain "to pray." And it is actually in this context, precisely while Jesus was *praying,* that "the appearance of his face was altered, and his clothing became a dazzling white" (Lk 9:28–29). What comes to mind is the face of Moses when he came down from the Mount of God. But here, Moses and Elijah, themselves passionate seekers of the face of God, are witnesses of the great light that emanates from the Lord Jesus.

The praying Jesus must have held a great fascination for his disciples, not only on the mount of the Transfiguration, but also elsewhere and on other occasions. For Luke, in fact, the prayer of the Our Father has its foundations in the admiration of the disciples. Seeing Jesus recollected in prayer, one of them draws near him and asks: "Lord, teach us to pray" (Lk 11:1).

Here the evangelist stops as though on a threshold. He tells us that Jesus is praying, but he keeps silent on the content of the prayer. The personal dialogue of Jesus with his Father unfolds in silence. Luke limits himself to stating the fact, allowing to grow within us, as it did in the disciple, the desire to learn: Lord, teach us to pray!

Sometimes—actually, three times in all—the silence gives way to words, and we are introduced into the intimacy of the personal relationship of the Son with the Father. This happens in a particular way during the terrible night of the passion, before Jesus' death.

The enemy, defeated in the battle that had taken place during the forty days in the desert (at which time Satan had devised "every kind of temptation"), had promised to return at "an opportune time" (Lk 4:13). Such was the time of the passion, in which Satan broke loose with all his strength and threatened to destroy the entire work of Jesus. Luke notes an increase in satanic activity from the beginning of chapter 22 with the imminence of the paschal meal, almost as if the entire story of the passion deals with the vigorous confrontation with evil. "Then Satan entered into Judas—the one called Iscariot—who was numbered among the twelve" (Lk 22:2). Not only is the person of Jesus in danger, but, more radically, so is his work. Of the twelve disciples, in fact, one of them will betray him, Peter will deny him, and the others will run away.

Jesus uses spiritual weapons to fight his battle against the powers of evil. First among them is prayer: "he withdrew about a stone's throw away from them, knelt down, and began to pray" (Lk 22:41; cf. also the fifth petition of the Our Father: Lk 11:4).

Luke prefers to emphasize the interior initiative of the Master; it is not the agony that has the upper hand but his will to pray. Jesus enters into the passion as an active protagonist; he goes into it "on his knees" before the Father: "Father, if it is your will, take this cup away from me, but not my will but yours be done" (v. 42).

As a just man who is being persecuted, Jesus seeks refuge from his torment in prayer: "Then there appeared to him an angel from heaven to strengthen him" (v. 43). The presence of a consoling angel demonstrates that God does not abandon one in the hour of trial. God is near and sustains the one who takes refuge in him. But God will not free Jesus from death. And although he sends an angel to comfort him, that does not stop the Son from experiencing anguish to the point of sweating blood:

> In his anguish he prayed more earnestly, and his sweat became like drops of blood falling to the ground (v. 44).

Jesus suffered the bitterness of death in all its fullness and felt its horrors in his own body. But the tempter did not succeed in taking from him his acceptance of the Father's will. The rest of Luke's account almost sounds like that of John; supported by prayer, Jesus goes to face his passion with the serenity of one who has the situation well in hand.

We find the word "Father" twice on the lips of the crucified Jesus. The first time he uses the word, Jesus is asking pardon for his brothers (23:34), and the second time Jesus is giving over to God his own life: "Father, into your hands I entrust my spirit" (23:46).

We are speaking here of the last words, of the final prayer of Jesus. They are also the words of Psalm 31, one of the psalms that devout rabbis suggest for prayer in the

evening. Luke sees the death of Jesus as a serene falling
asleep at night, waiting for the new morning. But there is
something new about the way Jesus prays the psalm. One
single word is sufficient to establish this newness: the title
Father.

Jesus dies entrusting himself to that Father who had
"occupied" his whole heart and his whole life. A great connection can be discerned between the first words that Jesus
pronounced in the Temple when he was twelve years old
and the last words on the cross.

> — "Did you not know that I had to concern myself with
>   my Father's affairs?" (Lk 2:49);
> — "Father, into your hands I entrust my spirit" (Lk 23:46).

In short, the entire life of Jesus, right up to his death on
the cross, can be seen under the sign of prayer and confidence in the Father. There is no doubt that this way of
living and dying exerted a powerful attraction and fascination on his circle of disciples, and Luke points this out well
enough. On our part we want to stop here and return to
the prayer of praise and wonder that flows from the heart
of Jesus, in his certainty that the Father reveals the mysteries of the Gospel to little ones and hides it from the presumptuous wise and clever.

I give you praise, O Father

The Master is caught up in a moment of interior exultation. He is speaking out loud, probably surrounded by
his disciples, but he is directly addressing the Father. It is

to him that Jesus turns, recognizing him as "the Lord of heaven and earth" and praising him for the fact that he hides from the wise and reveals himself to the little ones. Jesus is profoundly amazed with this fact and rejoices in it, acknowledging in this the Father's marvelous wisdom. He therefore reveals himself as the Son united to the Father in a perfect reciprocity of knowledge and love. And he declares that he is able to introduce his disciples into the same current of living knowledge.

Lk 10:21	*Mt 11:25–26*
"I praise you, Father,	"I praise you, Father,
Lord of heaven and earth,	Lord of heaven and earth,
because you hid	because you hid
from the wise	from the wise
and intelligent	and intelligent
and revealed them to babes;	and revealed them to babes;
yes, Father, for such was	yes, Father, for such was
your desire."	your desire."

This wonderful text, which we could call the "Magnificat of Jesus," is also present in Matthew in an identical form:

We want to dwell on this Scripture passage somewhat in order to gather its rich meaning, keeping in mind that this is the first and only time that the Lord Jesus spontaneously reveals his feelings of praise and wonder with regard to his Father.

It is typical of the Hebrew prayer of blessing (*berakah*) to praise God not in a general way but for something very concrete and specific. Even Jesus reflects this custom here. He turns to God, calling him Father and recognizing him as "Lord of heaven and of earth," yet he does not actually exalt him for his cosmic lordship. Jesus does not praise God because he created the heavens and the earth, but because "he hides and reveals" according to parameters that are entirely free and gratuitous.

Jesus blesses the Father for having hidden from the wise and revealed to the little ones "these things" (*tauta*). He doesn't specify what "these things" are, but he takes care to state clearly that this surprising upside-down situation (the ignorance of the wise and the knowledge of the little ones) reflects the approval, or rather the tastes, of his Father. This is true because the Father is pleased with it being this way (*eudokia egeneto*).

Eudokein underlines the loving and benign will of God; his mercy takes delight in the people he has chosen. The noun *eudokia* never appears in classic Greek, and Origen considered it a creation of biblical Greek. With it, the Septuagint almost always translates the Hebrew *rāsôn*, which means precisely the approval, the grace, the divine will. Now, precisely in mysteriously hiding knowledge from the wise and revealing it to the little ones, Jesus distinguishes the expression of the saving will of his Father, his tastes and his sovereign decision—that which he is pleased to do. Finally, Jesus reveals himself as the Son who has received the Father's confidence and has care of everything:

Lk 10:22	*Mt 11:27*
"All things have been given to me by my Father,	"All things have been given to me by my Father,
and no one knows who the Son is except the Father,	and no one knows the Son except the Father,
nor who the Father is except the Son,	nor does anyone know the Father except the Son,
and whoever the Son chooses	and whoever the Son chooses
to reveal him to."	to reveal him to."

All power has been given to Jesus, as the Wisdom of the Old Testament and as the Son of Man (cf. Dan 7:13–14: Enoc 1:38ff.; one also notices the connection with Mt 28:18 and with Jn 5:19–27). Only he knows the Father and only by the Father is he fully known, precisely as Wisdom (cf. Job 28:23–27; Wis 8:3–4; 9:9). Besides, Jesus has the power to communicate knowledge of the Father and of himself to whomever he wishes. He is the Son who with complete freedom and authority carries the supreme revelation of the mystery of God.

But what specifically has the Father hidden and revealed? In and of itself, the text does not say. If we want to figure out the meaning of *tauta* ("these things"), we then have to question the text, above all the preceding one, inasmuch as it contains the concrete reasons that are the foundation of Jesus' rejoicing. Analyzing the texts of Matthew and Luke, we are aware that the words of Jesus are introduced from different viewpoints. Consequently, what the Father keeps hidden or reveals takes on different shades in the two versions.

The Matthean context

In Matthew what the Father has hidden are "the things" (*tauta*) regarding the evangelization of Jesus, which was refused by the cities around the Lake of Galilee (Chorazin, Bethsaida, Capernaum). In fact, Jesus' joy is preceded by an invective, a denunciation in prophetic tones: the "woe" against the unrepentant cities.

The following context illustrates the situation, which explains well the reversal of which the prayer speaks. The little ones to whom the Father is pleased to reveal "these things" seem to be identified with the disciples of Jesus. Our text would therefore find at the center of these opposing situations:

— on the one hand, the unrepentant towns and, more broadly, "this generation," which does not recognize in the works of Jesus the sign of his being the Messiah (Mt 11:2–24);

— on the other hand, the disciples to whom it is given to understand the mysteries of the Kingdom of God and the things hidden from the foundation of the world (Mt 13:1–17).

With their stubbornness, the lake cities seem to have greatly frustrated the ministry of Jesus. At Chorazin, Bethsaida, and above all in Capernaum, the Master had invested much apostolic energy. He preached more in these cities, worked a greater number of healings there, and, in short, had dedicated to them his time, patience, and prayer. Having given so much, he waited for a corresponding response, the "fruits of conversion." Instead, he had to learn that no positive response would come and that it was precisely these cities that put up the greatest resistance to his Word....

But lack of success did not discourage Jesus or impede his confidence. He lived his mission in profound dialogue with the Father and interpreted everything in light of that relationship. Thus what according to human reasoning simply resulted in failure and lack of apostolic success acquired a new dimension, in which even setbacks might somehow enter into the divine will.

In effect, by introducing Jesus' confession of praise immediately after his bitter observation about the lake towns' lack of correspondence, Matthew also suggests an interpretation that Jesus makes regarding his own mission. The incomprehension on the part of those cities that had benefited the most from his miracles allowed Jesus to grasp the mysterious presence of his Father. A profound reason exists at the bottom of their refusal. There is a presumptuous wisdom, a subtle pride in one who is "familiar" with the divine world.... And so, from the presumably wise and intelligent ones, the Father has hidden the profound meaning of the Gospel ("these things"). He has revealed it instead to the "little ones," who are represented by the disciples: "To you it is given to know the secrets of the Kingdom of heaven, but to them it is not given" (Mt 13:11).

The Lucan context

The third evangelist offers a new context as compared to Matthew. Luke places a break between the "woes" of Jesus against the unrepentant cities (Lk 10:13–15) and his "rejoicing" over the work of the Father (10:21–22) with the return of the seventy-two disciples (vv. 17–20).

In this way Luke indicates a connection between Jesus' joy and his collaborators' evangelizing work. The disciples return to him "full of joy," above all because they experienced that even the demons were subject to them in his name.

Jesus replies that he has seen Satan fall "like lightning from heaven"; and so the devil's defeat coincides with the coming of the Kingdom. As for his disciples, Jesus has given them the power to face even the most insidious dangers ("the power to walk on snakes and scorpions") without, however, suffering any harm ("nothing will be able to harm you"). But he adds that there is a much more profound reason for joy: "Do not rejoice in the fact that the spirits are subject to you—rejoice because your names are recorded in heaven" (v. 20).

At this point Luke introduces the joy of Jesus with a particular insight that is absent in Matthew; he notes that Jesus "rejoiced [*egalliasato*] in the Holy Spirit."

This verb was already on the lips of Mary in her Magnificat: "My spirit rejoices [*egalliasen*] in God my Savior" (Lk 1:47). For the third evangelist, Spirit and prayer—above all the prayer of praise and rejoicing—go together. Besides the canticle of Mary, we remember also that of Elizabeth, "full of the Holy Spirit," and the rejoicing of the infant John in the womb of his mother (Lk 1:41–44).

Now it is Jesus who in the Spirit rejoices with uncontainable joy and breaks forth into a confession of praise: "I praise you, Father" (*exomologoumai soi, pater...*). Jesus' words are exactly the same in Luke and Matthew. They are introduced, however, from different perspectives, and this is not inconsequential with regard to their interpretation.

In a certain sense Matthew seems struck by the humiliation of the proud ("woe" to the cities who haven't listened), while Luke seems more impressed by the exultation of the little ones (the seventy-two who return full of joy). The exultation due to this reversal brought about by the Father is prolonged in the beatitudes that Jesus pronounces over the disciples. The Master turns directly to them and proclaims them blessed (see Lk 10:23–24).

They are the fortunate recipients of the Father's kindness and of his revelation. It has been granted to their eyes to see what many before them had longed to see but did not. But the true beatitude of Jesus' disciples lies precisely in the gift of seeing beyond, which is granted to the little ones and concealed from the wise.

Jesus, the little one who welcomes the revelation of the Father

It has already been said that this prayer could be titled the Magnificat of Jesus. The prayer is a spontaneous effusion, a joy of the soul expressed with identical words in Matthew and in Luke. This is something highly significant. Not even the "Our Father," the prayer that Jesus taught his disciples after they requested this of him, sounds the same in the two Gospels. This "spontaneous praise" is precisely the only prayer of Jesus transmitted in exactly the same way by both evangelists (Mt 11:25–26; Lk 10:21).

Through this spontaneous praise we are invited beyond the threshold into the filial dialogue of Jesus with his Father. The two are in profound harmony. If Jesus is the evangelizer, the Father is the revealer. It is impossible to accept Jesus if the Father does not reveal the definitive meaning of the Gospel. As John says: "No one can come to me unless it is given by the Father" (6:65).

But there is more. In reflecting on his own experience, and in constant dialogue with his Father, Jesus discovers that reversal of situations that characterizes the divine intervention in the history of Israel, that radical about-face of which Mary sang in her Magnificat: "He has...scattered the arrogant in the conceit of their heart; he has pulled down the mighty from their thrones, and exalted the lowly..." (Lk 1:51–52).

And so, the experience of which Jesus sings is fairly close to that of his Mother. They sing of what they have personally experienced. As his mother before him, Jesus also is one of the poor and simple who is exalted. In fact, it is to him above all that "these things" have been revealed by the Father, while he has hidden them from the wise. Rich in the revelation that his Father has given to him, Jesus can now declare aloud and before the disciples who have trusted in his words that it will always be so. It will always be to the little ones—to those who are childlike, to the simple of mind and heart—that the Father will reveal the mysteries of the Kingdom.

CHAPTER 8

The teaching of Jesus in parables

*T*here is no doubt that among the different forms of teaching, Jesus preferred teaching in parables. The parables are brief, animated stories from everyday life. They dynamically involve their listeners, challenging them personally and arousing them to critical judgment on the situation being presented and, implicitly, on the reality to which the parable alludes. The parable, in fact, functions when the one who listens is able to grasp the fundamental intuition or decisive point of the story; it then releases the mechanism that launches its listeners "beyond the parable" toward the reality intended by the storyteller.

Something of this launching mechanism is suggested by the word itself. The Greek *parabolé* is composed of the preposition *para*, which means "nearby," and the word *bolé*, which comes from the verb *ballein* ("to throw, to launch") and means "a shot" (of stone). *Parabolé* could mean either a fleet of ships side by side, a conjunction of planets, or a comparison between two situations....

The parable is based on an analogy—that is, on an approach whereby a fictitious account is presented and compared with an element of reality, the reason for which the storyteller has invented the story.[2]

The parable's phenomenon is therefore not to be found in the story in and of itself, but rather in the dynamic comparison of two things: the story and the reality to which it refers. A parable, observes J. Dupont, never contains within itself its complete meaning; it "cannot have meaning apart from its relation to a *something beyond*."[3]

This function of transferal is well illustrated in the parable the prophet Nathan tells to King David after his sin with Bathsheba and the murder of her husband, Uriah:

> "There were two men in a certain city, the one rich and the other poor. The rich man had very many flocks and herds; but the poor man had nothing but one little ewe lamb, which he had bought. He brought it up, and it grew up with him and with his children; it used to eat of his meager fare, and drink from his cup, and lie in his bosom, and it was like a daughter to him. Now there came a traveler to the rich man, and he was loath to take one of his own flock or herd to prepare for the wayfarer who had come to him, but he took the poor man's lamb, and prepared that for the guest who had come to him." Then David's anger was greatly kindled against the man. He said to Nathan, "As the LORD lives, the man who has done this deserves to die; he shall restore the lamb fourfold, because he did this thing, and because he had no pity." Nathan said to David: "You are the man!" (2 Sam 12:1–7)

2. Cf. V. Fusco, *Oltre la parabola* (Rome 1983), 68 ff.

3. J. Dupont, *Il metodo parabolico di Gesù* (Brescia 1978), 7.

Here is an effective parable! David follows with attention—more, he is completely caught up in the story, so much so that he takes an immediate position and utters a just sentence. He has identified with it to such an extent that he is not even aware of how transparent the event just narrated is: "You are that man!"

In order to understand the parables of Jesus it is important to identify the *historical occasions* that generated them or, rather, what impelled Jesus to invent a given account. If we succeed in discovering the occasion that gave birth to the parable, we will be in the best position to make the leap to the *reality* that was *intended* in the first place.

This is not as easy as it would seem at first glance, since in handing down the parables of Jesus the evangelists often took them out of their original context—that is, from the historical occasion in which Jesus told the parable—and inserted them into new contexts and occasions, suggested by the concrete situations of their own communities.

It is from these contexts and given this evangelical editing that we must begin. From here we attempt to climb, not without fatigue and some difficulty, to the original level, that is, to the parable's context in the ministry of Jesus. I propose such a course as regards the well-known parable, handed down to us both in Matthew and in Luke, of the shepherd and the lost sheep.

We will dedicate this lectio to allowing ourselves to be evangelized by this delightful parable, which reveals to us in an eminent way the face of God in Jesus Christ. We ask for the grace to experience something of the joy of God for our salvation and of being capable of sincere joy over the conversion of our brothers and sisters.

The parables of great joy

Luke situates the three parables of chapter 15, defined as "the Gospel of mercy," in the context of the great journey Jesus makes toward Jerusalem. The parables share the theme of the joy of God for the converted sinner.

Joy, this extraordinary emotion of God, is illustrated by three figures: the shepherd who rejoices over having found his lost sheep (vv. 4–7); the woman who has turned her house upside down to search for a lost coin, and, after finding it, calls in her friends and neighbors to rejoice with her (vv. 8–10); and, finally, the joy of the father for the son who was lost and is found again (vv. 11–32).

The first two verses of chapter 15 comprise the "narrative frame" for these three parables. The Master is surrounded by publicans and sinners while, at a certain distance, the leaders of Israel murmur.

Jesus exercises a strong attraction on the publicans and sinners, whom the Pharisees contemptuously call "people of the earth" (*'am ha 'arez*) and consider incapable and unworthy of the Word of God. But here, in strong contrast, we see them interested in Jesus' words: "The tax collectors and sinners were all drawing near to listen to him." They form a circle around Jesus. They feel understood by him rather than judged, and for this reason they approach him with confidence.

At a proper distance stands a second circle of people. These are the scribes and Pharisees, who as usual are "murmuring." The Greek verb used by the evangelist, *diegòngyzon,* seems almost to reproduce the sound of a whisper, of a rising discontent. And so the grumbling is articulated: "This fellow welcomes sinners and eats with them."

"To eat" with someone is undoubtedly a sign of solidarity. A banquet is spoken of both in the preceding passage (Lk 14:21–24) and at the end of this same chapter, which speaks of the feast organized by the father for the son who was lost and is found again. The Pharisees' accusation seems out of place here. Publicans and sinners are actually coming close to Jesus not "to eat" with him as much as "to listen to him." In any case, although within a literary context this accusation proves to be out of place, in the historical context it corresponds to truth. When Jesus later invites himself to the house of Zacchaeus, Luke notes that everyone "complained" (the same verb): "He has gone to a sinner's house" (Lk 19:7).

Jesus is therefore at the center of the scene, sought by one group and accused by another. He observes, listens, and finally responds to the indignant complaints of those who believe themselves "just." He answers with three parables, of which the first is noted also in Matthew (18:12–14). But the story is different in that context, as is the viewpoint from which it is told. While in Luke the figure of the shepherd illustrates the behavior of God—and, when all is said and done, that of Jesus—Matthew instead points out the behavior of the Church, the responsibility of each for one's own brother or sister.

To better understand the similarities and differences, we can compare the two texts.

Mt 18:12–14	*Lk 15:4–7*
"What do you think? If a man has a hundred sheep and one of them strays away, won't he leave the ninety- nine on the mountainside and go look for the one that went astray? And if he happens to find it,	"What man among you who had a hundred sheep and lost one of them would not leave the ninety- nine in the desert and set out after the lost one *until* he found it?
I say to you, he *rejoices* over it more than over the ninety-nine that didn't go astray.	And when he finds it he puts it on his shoulders, *rejoicing,* and when he comes home he calls his friends and neigh- bors together and says to them, *'Rejoice with me*—I have found my lost sheep.'
Likewise, it is not the will of your Father in heaven that one of these little ones should be lost."	I say to you that this is the type of *joy* there will be in heaven at the repentance of one sinner, rather than at ninety- nine of the righteous who had no need of repentance."

The Matthean context

Matthew places the parable of the lost sheep in the context of the communitarian discourse (chapter 18), from the perspective of the "little ones" of the community.

The "ecclesial context" is well emphasized by the specific vocabulary of this chapter. Twice in verse 17 we find the word *ekklesia*, "assembly," "church"—a word that occurs nowhere else in the Gospels—and from the beginning of verse 15 we find the word *adelphos*, "brother."

The composition of this discourse is well planned; everything revolves around three questions asked respectively by the disciples (18:1), by Jesus (18:12), and by Peter (18:21).

Each of the questions is answered in a parable. The disciples' question deals with a crucial point: "Who is the greatest in the Kingdom of heaven?" Jesus responds with an eloquent gesture, with a parable-in-action: he places a child "in the midst of them," and to avoid any misunderstanding he adds: "Unless you turn about and become like children, you will never enter the Kingdom of heaven."

The Master's words completely upset the standards of greatness common in the society of that day (and in our day as well): the greatest in the Kingdom is the one who humbles him or herself. And whoever does not accept "becoming like children" will end up "staying outside"; that person will not be worthy even to "enter."

From this symbolic gesture of Jesus—the child placed in the midst of his disciples—Matthew goes on to speak of "the little ones" and recounts a series of warnings to safeguard the rights of the weak. In the Christian community the strong should not prevail over the weak; rather, there should be thoughtful attention given to the "little ones" (vv. 6–14).

But who were these "little ones" (*mikroi toutoi*)?

They were probably Christians still weak and fragile in faith, exposed for different reasons to "scandals"—that is, to the possibility of tripping up and falling. Perhaps, because of their weakness, they might be taken in by someone and, consequently, find themselves far from the fold....

Precisely because they are little, these believers should be defended and loved in a particular way. It would be better to experience a tragic end than to cause scandal to even one of these little ones who believes in Jesus (vv. 6–7). The community should be careful not to look down on them (v. 10) and, more positively, should express solicitude in their regard, the kind of solicitude illustrated in the parable of the shepherd who searches for the lost sheep.

What do you think?

Matthew introduces this parable with a question meant to directly involve the listeners (the same question also introduces the parable of the murderous vinedressers: cf. Mt 21:28). Jesus presents the case of a man who, having a hundred sheep, realizes that one of them is missing. What will this man do?

Matthew describes the action in two connecting instances:

1. He will certainly leave the ninety-nine on the mountain and go in search of (*zetei*) the wandering sheep. The sheep's condition is described with the verb *planao*, which means "to wander about," to go roaming, to lose oneself.

2. If he succeeds in finding it (the missing sheep could also end up in the mouth of a ferocious beast or in the hands of a thief), he will "rejoice" more over this one than over the ninety-nine who did not go astray.

In this passage, the initial question ("What do you think?") lets us understand that the listeners agree. Jesus can therefore finish his parable "going beyond," suggesting a similar relationship ("and so") between the behavior of the shepherd and that of God: "Likewise, it is not the will of your Father in heaven that one of these little ones should be lost" (Mt 18:14). As the shepherd cannot resign himself to the loss of his little sheep, so God does not want even one of these little ones to be lost.

Paradoxically, that sheep seems to be worth more than the other ninety-nine from the moment that the shepherd is ready to "leave them" in order to recover "the wandering one." If he finds it, his joy is greater than the contentment he would feel in having the other ninety-nine safe.

All of this is to emphasize how important this sheep is to the shepherd. The conclusion of the parable makes an obvious connection between the wandering sheep and the condition of the "little ones." The parable resonates in the "ecclesial" context of Matthew 18 and, therefore, is meant to illustrate behavior in the heart of the community. The "little ones" should be the object of special attention. If one of them strays, then we have to set out in search of that one before all is lost.

The parable of the lost sheep is noted also in the Gospel of Thomas, a Coptic apocryphal gospel, which has variations that differ considerably from the evangelical meaning. According to the Gospel of Thomas, the lost sheep is "the biggest," and when the shepherd finds it he says: "I love you more than the other ninety-nine!" This sheep is the strongest and most beautiful, which is the reason for the shepherd's preference (I, 107).

It is exactly the opposite in Matthew, where it is precisely the smallest that should be the object of particular care and attention.

The parable according to Luke

For Luke the situation of the sheep is much more serious than in Matthew: it is not only "wandering," but is already "lost." To illustrate the situation of this sheep, the third evangelist does not use the verb *planao* (as Matthew does), but the verb *apollymi*, which more radically underlines the seriousness of its condition.

But Luke nonetheless has no doubts that the shepherd will recover his sheep. In fact, while in Matthew there is a certain reservation, an "if" that leaves us in suspense of the search's outcome, Luke takes away this dramatic "if"; he is certain of success, certain that the shepherd will find his lost sheep.

Luke does not use the verb "to search"; however, more than Matthew, he underlines the care that the shepherd takes in searching. In fact, the shepherd does not stop his tireless search "until he [has] found it" (15:4).

Finally, more than Matthew, Luke distinguishes the joy of the shepherd. He not only rejoices when he finds his sheep but also rejoices afterward. When he arrives home, he calls his friends and neighbors in for a feast: "Rejoice with me—I have found my lost sheep!" (15:6)

Luke's portrayal of the parable greatly emphasizes the Christological perspective and well supports what the evangelist means to communicate. Luke emphasizes how Jesus' behavior reveals the extreme mercy of the Father for those who are far from him and for sinners, for the "lost." Jesus reveals the extraordinary joy of God in the conversion of sinners. This divine capacity "to rejoice and celebrate" is described as a necessity: "But we had to celebrate and rejoice—this brother of yours was dead, and has come back to life, he was lost, and has been found" (Lk 15:32). The Church of Jesus Christ must never forget such extraordinary divine emotion!

The inspiration found in Ezekiel 34

Both in the text of Matthew as well as in that of Luke, the parable is based on Ezekiel 34:1–16. The oracle of the prophet announces the severe judgment of YHWH against the shepherds of Israel who pasture themselves instead of the sheep (vv. 2–10). The shepherds have betrayed their duty, not paying attention to the weak, the poor, and the needy. The prophet exposes a sequence of omissions:

you have not strengthened the weak,
you have not bound up the injured,
you have not brought back the strayed,
you have not sought the lost (34:4).

But in contrast to the wickedness of the shepherds there is the work of YHWH. The Lord himself will shepherd his people (34:11–16); he will search for his sheep; he will take care of them and gather them from all the nations:

I will seek the lost,
and I will bring back the strayed (34:16a).

It is curious to note how both Matthew and Luke draw from this verse, respectively selecting, however, only one of the two terms used by Ezekiel. Matthew defines the sheep as "wandering" (*to planomenon*), while Luke presents it as "lost" (*to apololos*).

From Matthew's viewpoint, the sinner is not someone who is "lost" but rather "wandering." The duty of the shepherd, of the one who has ecclesial responsibility, is to go and search for the sheep with all possible solicitude. If the shepherd succeeds in finding the sheep, there will be joy because the salvific will of the Father is accomplished. All of this is in thematic continuity with the rest of the ecclesial discourse: "If your brother should sin [against you], go show him his error between you and him alone. If he listens to you, you have won your brother back" (Mt 18:15).

Luke instead sees the sinner not merely as one who has lost the way or gone astray, but as one who is more radically "lost." Far from the fold and from the shepherd, the sheep becomes easy prey for any wild beast, as is observed in the oracle of Ezekiel (34:5–8).

By taking care of sinners, Jesus fulfills the prophecy of Ezekiel 34. Publicans and sinners are the sheep who are sick, abandoned, and lost, treated harshly by the shepherds of Israel (the scribes and Pharisees) who do not love their company and want to banish them far from the flock. Jesus, on the contrary, seeks the company of sinners, is their "doctor," and "eats with them" (cf. Mt 2:15–17).

When he enters the house of Zacchaeus, there are still some who complain and murmur, but Jesus declares openly: "The Son of man came to seek out and save what was lost" (Lk 19:10). And so the meaning of the parable is clear. Jesus is the Good Shepherd, who goes in search of the lost one "until he finds it."

The art of telling parables

Jesus knew the art of discreetly involving the person. In essence the parable is a *dialogical* form that was used in order to overcome the listener's resistance. If Jesus had spoken openly about the Kingdom, he would have been immediately contested; therefore, he used the enigmatic language of the parable, with which one generally addressed adversaries or dissenters in order to capture their assent.

With the "parabolic" discourse, or slant, of a fictitious story, Jesus threw across a bridge to produce an understanding in his listeners, to arouse them to make a decision. Such, however, depends on one's free assent. But in the meantime, Jesus, with a keen pedagogical touch, offered the possibility of such an assent.

Luke, more than any other evangelist, emphasizes the mercy of Jesus toward sinners. In the synagogue of Nazareth the Master interpreted his mission as one destined to give liberty to the oppressed and to open the doors to those imprisoned, since God has decided to give his grace to all. But not everyone looked at this mission in the same way. Some were indignant that the Master transgressed religious conventions and was friendly with sinners. They allowed him to heal the sick, to cure the lepers, and to give sight to the blind (always stipulating that this didn't take place on a Sabbath, of course), but they became affronted if he directed his therapeutic action to those who were sick in spirit, if he was familiar with sinners, if he spoke of God to prostitutes....

And so Jesus was forced to *defend himself.* Evangelizing the scribes and Pharisees must have seemed more arduous than evangelizing sinners....

How could he "evangelize" the scribes and Pharisees who were "complaining" about his behavior? Not directly, but by telling three parables that describe in an appealing manner the way God is and the way God acts. Jesus seems to reason thus: "*You* tell *me:* which method comes closer to the behavior of God—yours or mine?" Jesus does not like having to defend himself. Let his listeners draw their own conclusions!

The parables constitute, then, a *discrete form of evangelization,* providing a stepping stone or a rope to the listeners so that they themselves can reflect, judge, and draw their conclusions. In that sense the parable does not offer beautiful, ready-made solutions; rather, it offers questions and provocations: What do you think? Which one of you will respond? What will one do?

The listener must also pronounce the judgment. Think of the story Jesus invents in the house of Simon the Pharisee: "A certain creditor had two debtors...which of them will love him more?" Simon does not hesitate in pronouncing his point of view: "I suppose the one he forgave the most." And Jesus comes back with: "You have judged correctly" (see Lk 7:31–50).

At this point the second part of the parable begins. Once the desired response is obtained, Jesus returns to the present situation: "Do you see this woman...?" The fictitious story allows the speaker to pronounce a free and detached judgment, which he would not be disposed to formulate directly about the situation. Our Pharisee, in fact, reasons about Jesus this way in his heart: "If this fellow were a prophet he would realize who and what kind of woman it is who is touching him—she is a sinner" (v. 39). If Jesus had told him directly that this woman surpassed him in love, Simon probably would have held fast to his position. The strategy of the parable is to make the "judgment" or "conclusion" desired by the storyteller flow from the very same listener.

Parables are actually a discrete form of evangelization—not only for sinners, but also, and perhaps above all, for their adversaries.

The women miraculously cured by Jesus

*I*n his missionary journeys at the side of the Apostle Paul, Luke must have often experienced the generous welcome and strong charism of certain Christian women —intelligent, capable, energetic women who opened their homes to the itinerant missionaries and who supported the cause of the Gospel through their love and dedication (see the figure of Lydia in Ac 16:15), just as Martha and Mary had done for Jesus (Lk 10:38–42).

Luke was also aware of a certain continuity between "then" (the time of Jesus) and "now" (the time of the early Church). For our evangelist the time of the Spirit opened new horizons as much for women as for men.

Jesus established himself as liberator and healer of the whole of humanity, both male and female. Luke is attentive to this novelty and frequently features a man with a woman in the parables or in the stories of healing. So the parable of the shepherd who goes in search of his lost sheep is coupled with the housewife who searches for her lost coin; and the healing of the man possessed by the demon in the synagogue of Capernaum finds a certain correspondence in the healing of Simon's mother-in-law. Jesus rebukes the strange fever that had imprisoned the woman exactly as he had rebuked the demon shortly before (the same verb is used, *epetimesen:* Lk 4:35, 39). In this way Luke creates a parallel structure that highlights the attention Jesus gives to all reality, masculine and feminine.

The Savior has come to free men and women, both of whom are blocked, oppressed, self-enslaved, and imprisoned in the cell of their own ignorance, egoism, and death. The healings he works show his solidarity more than exalt his power. He is the Servant of the Lord who takes upon himself our sicknesses and infirmities. In him, God has truly visited and redeemed his people (see Lk 1:68).

But how do these healings take place? Is it enough to simply be sick and ask the grace of being healed by Jesus? Luke emphasizes that healing and salvation are also an option, a personal choice, bound to the dynamic of faith, of risk, and of love. Undoubtedly the fundamental aspect of healing lies in the gratuitous divine initiative. Jesus shows to the greatest extent God's solidarity with men and women who are suffering, who are oppressed by evil and by different kinds of sickness. He reveals in a vibrant way the compassion God feels for suffering humanity, and he presents himself as physician and Savior. He actualizes what his name signifies: *Savior*, the concrete expression of the divine will to offer grace, to heal, and to restore. Nonetheless, Luke emphasizes a second aspect, inseparable from the first: the human condition that makes healing possible. Salvation comes from faith, humility, and love.

The Savior met many women on his journeys, and many had benefited from his healing energy. In the third Gospel we encounter a symbolic number of seven women for whom Jesus works miracles of physical, psychic, and spiritual healing. Two of these women are directly involved in miracles of resurrection: the widow of Nain, for whom Jesus restored her only son, and the young daughter of Jairus.

Of these seven women, only one is called by name: Mary of Magdala, "liberated from seven demons" (Lk 8:2). Of her, first on the list of itinerant women disciples, we have already spoken in chapter 6. Here we will dedicate our attention to the other six women, who are presented not by name, but based on their social and parental condition, or, rather, in relationship to a certain man: mother-in-law of, daughter of, widow of. Paradoxically, this meager remembrance of individual femininity could also have a positive aspect. And that is the fact that the Gospel is silent regarding the proper name of the woman so that the healing may be seen in light of her relationship with "man" (mother-in-law, mother, daughter, widow). This could be read as an allusive or symbolic healing of mutual health, which involves the good and the joy of the whole family.

The mother-in-law of Peter,
or the healing for service

The first miracle Jesus accomplishes for a woman has as its protagonist Simon's mother-in-law. All three of the synoptics refer to the event, and this is already an indication of its importance. Luke, following the plot narrated by Mark, presents several miracles, beginning with those for a man and a woman respectively.

We are at Capernaum, a city situated on the northeast edge of Lake Gennesaret, (in Hebrew *Kinneret*, a name alluding to its shape, which resembles a harp or lyre, *kinnor*). It is the Sabbath and Jesus spends the morning in the synagogue, impressing the people with the authority of his teaching and with his power over demons. In fact, he frees a man who was imprisoned by evil, and those present are in awe of it: "What is this? A new teaching—with authority! He commands even the unclean spirits, and they obey him" (Lk 4:36). Leaving the synagogue, Jesus enters the house of Peter, where another uncomfortable situation awaits him: "Simon's mother-in-law was suffering from a high fever" (v. 38). Unlike Mark, who simply has the disciples introduce the situation to the Master ("and at once they told Jesus about her": Mk 1:30), Luke immediately underscores the dimension of prayer: "and they appealed to him on her account."

Jesus grants the prayer of the family. He draws close to the bed and kneels down by the sick woman. Yet it isn't to the woman that he addresses himself, but rather to the fever, almost as though it were an animated reality, a demon. Jesus rebukes and threatens the fever, which immediately obeys him and leaves. The woman is now free of the evil that had kept her in bed; she can get up by herself and give proof of her healing as she starts to serve those present (see Lk 4:38–39).

It is easy to see the symbolic value of these healings: Jesus takes care of the man and the woman, liberating both from what holds them imprisoned and restoring them to their livelihood. He works wonders and miracles not only in public but also in private, within the walls of one's home. Liberated from this strange fever, Simon's mother-in-law again finds joy in gracious and generous service of those in the house and of her new guest and benefactor. This readiness "to put oneself at service"—something forbidden by rabbis, who prohibited women from "serving at the table"—most likely is already "an indication of the new duties which wait for women in the Christian community."[4]

The widow of Nain

The second miracle that Jesus works for a woman is told in Luke 7:11–17. We are at the gates of the city of Nain, which tradition places on the slopes of Tabor. "...He went to a city called Nain, and his disciples and a large crowd went with him." At the gate of the city a funeral is taking place. It is always sad to accompany a funeral cortege, but

---

4. H. Schürmann, *Il vangelo di Luca* (Brescia: 1983), 434.

here the situation is particularly serious. The deceased was "his mother's only son, and she was a widow." Many people from the city are with her. Seeing her, the Lord *has compassion* (*esplanchnisthe*). The Greek verb Luke uses to describe the sentiments of Jesus indicates a strong emotion, coming from the very bowels (*splancha*) and taking over the person almost to the point of the loss of rational control. It is visceral and passionate emotion, involving the entire person. "Don't cry!" Jesus says to that poor mother. But what do such words mean to a mother who is accompanying her only son to the cemetery? They are empty words, absolutely insensitive. The evangelist does not refer to the woman's reaction, however; he concentrates on Jesus' behavior: "Then he came forward and touched the bier and the bearers stood still, and he said, 'Young man, I say to you, arise!'"

What happens next is completely unexpected: "The dead man sat up and began to speak" (a comparison with the resurrection of the son of the widow of Zarephath shows the superiority of Jesus over Elijah: cf. 1 Kings 17:19–24). But Jesus has not finished. The action must be seen in relation to its source. This powerful miracle, worked with only the power of his word, was born from compassion for that widowed mother who was crying. The young man is not simply "resurrected"; Jesus restores him as a son—"and Jesus gave him to his mother"—so that the woman would find again her meaning in life and the joy of living it still.

The reader's thoughts will jump spontaneously to another woman: the Mother of Jesus. Her only Son would even be denied an adequate tomb. As for Jesus, he has revealed to us his weak point: he does not know how to resist the tears of a mother. His weakness coincides with the same compassion of God. This is the conclusion that the inhabitants of Nain reached that day, as well as the disciples of Jesus and the whole crowd who enthusiastically exclaimed: "God has visited his people!" (Lk 7:16)

The woman with a hemorrhage and the daughter of Jairus

The third story we find in Luke 8:41–56, where the evangelist interweaves two miracles: the healing of a woman who had suffered the loss of blood for twelve years (Lk 8:43–48) and the resurrection of the twelve-year-old daughter of Jairus. The figure of the latter is inseparably bound to that of her father (the only person whose name is given to us), Jairus, which in Hebrew means "God shines." And undoubtedly, through Jesus, God shines on this passionate father. He is a prominent man, with a certain social status, who is "head of the synagogue." Jairus has an only daughter for whom he must have had a special affection. A daughter of twelve years who is now dying. In his grief this father turns to Jesus, throws himself at his feet as a slave before his master, and begs Jesus to return with him to his house. He pays no regard for his reputation; the only thing that matters at that moment is the life of his daughter. Jesus agrees to go with him and cure her.

> ...As Jesus slowly made his way, the crowd kept pressing in on him. A woman was there who had had a heavy flow of

blood for twelve years. She [had spent her whole livelihood
on doctors but] could not be cured by anyone. She came up
and touched the tassel of his cloak from behind, and immediately the flow of blood stopped (Lk 8:43–44).

This miracle is also noted in Mark, who describes the
situation with a somewhat cutting remark: this woman
had spent her whole inheritance consulting doctors who
proved ineffective, and she was now reduced to misery.
Luke, whom tradition presents to us as a doctor, perhaps
wanted to spare his profession from insult; he omits that
particular reference. He limits himself to mentioning, and
it is more than sufficient to imagine, the sad reality of the
protagonist, that "no one could cure her." Humiliated by
her sickness, which rendered her "impure" (cf. Lev
15:19–27), the woman hoped to pass unobserved. It was
enough for her to touch "the tassel of his cloak" (only Luke
refers to this particular detail).

The miracle seems destined to sit in the shadows,
known only by her who with much faith touches the "tassel" of his mantle. In her humility this woman does not
want to bother the Master, but she has such faith in Jesus
as to believe that only the slightest contact with his clothes
will be able to heal her.

But Jesus is aware of her and decides to make the
woman's gesture public. "Who was it that touched me?" he
asks the crowd that tightly encircles him. No one acknowledges doing so, but still Jesus insists. Peter justifiably marvels that the Master can even ask such a question, and he
pointedly observes: "Master, the crowd is pressing in on you

and crowding around." Jesus persists, however: "Someone touched me—I could feel power going out from me." Then the woman, realizing that she cannot remain hidden, comes forward trembling and throws herself at his feet.... And the "someone" who touched the Lord is revealed to be a woman. In a much different way than the crowd, she touched him with great faith. And she found herself healed.

Jesus turns to the woman with tenderness; he calls her "daughter" (*thigàter*). Between the two there is already a profound connection. For Jesus, this woman is not simply one among many; she is unique and he wants to "know" her face. It is impossible not to recognize a daughter! He is on his way to restore the only daughter of Jairus and, along the way, he encounters and heals another daughter. "Daughter, your faith has saved you; go in peace!" (v. 48)

While Jesus "was still speaking," someone from the synagogue leader's house reaches them quickly to inform Jairus: "Your daughter has died; do not trouble the teacher further" (Lk 8:49). The words are spoken only to the father, very quietly. But Jesus, who moments earlier had felt the delicate touch of the woman, sees the sad news reflected in Jairus' face. And immediately he encourages the grief-stricken father: "Don't be afraid. Just believe and she will be saved" (v. 50).

When they arrive at the house, they find everyone "weeping and mourning for her"—a ritual weeping, as dictated for an only daughter taken prematurely from life. Jesus tells them not to cry, because "she has not died, she is sleeping" (v. 52). Those present are cynical: *Try to tell others that the young girl is "sleeping," we've seen her!* "And they laughed at him because they knew she had died" (v. 53).

In the presence of only the girl's parents and of Peter, John, and James (who will witness his transfiguration: Lk 9:28), Jesus then approaches the young girl, takes her hand, and commands her in a loud voice: "Child, arise!" The resulting resurrection is immediate: "Her spirit returned and she immediately sat up" (vv. 54–55).

Her parents are dumbfounded, unable to believe their own eyes. Jesus, the derided dreamer, brings them gently back to reality, inviting them to give their little girl something to eat. And he hands the child back to her parents, as he had done earlier with the widow of Nain, so that they can take care of her and find in this their joy. By now, these people are witnesses that Jesus has overcome the supreme evil: death.

The woman crippled for eighteen years

We find a third story of healing in Luke 13:10–17. The miracle takes place on a Sabbath, within a synagogue, exactly like the first miracle Jesus accomplished in Capernaum for a possessed man (Lk 4:33–36). In this case it is a woman who is dominated by the sickness, its prisoner for eighteen years. This woman is extremely "bent over."

Specialists speak of "hysterical scoliosis," a severe folding over upon oneself, such that the back curves in a spasmodic way: "She was bent over double and unable to straighten herself up fully" (Lk 13:11).

No one introduces her to the Master. She personally does not put forward any prayer. She is simply there, bent over. Notwithstanding her malady she is present, in that synagogue, as she probably was every Sabbath. This woman has suffered patiently for a long time: eighteen years (representing a symbolic number of fullness: 3 x 6); and, in spite of her illness, she still comes often to the synagogue. She has, therefore, maintained her faith and her confidence in the Lord of life.

"When Jesus saw her, he called out to her and said, 'Woman, you have been set free from your illness.' Then he laid his hands on her and she straightened up immediately and began glorifying God" (Lk 13:12–13). Now the woman is free, upright, as a human being should be. She is finally able to look up to heaven and "give praise to God."

But someone else is not happy with this physical-psychological healing, namely, the head of the synagogue, who berates the people who have come to be cured on a Sabbath. He is too cowardly to directly attack Jesus (after all, one never knows; it doesn't pay to make enemies of a healer!), it is better to rage against the people: "There are six days on which it is proper to perform work, so come be healed on those days, and not on the Sabbath."

That poor woman, who had not asked for anything and whom Jesus has just healed, would probably have continued to praise God, without giving too much weight to such indignation. But Jesus takes up her defense and that of all the oppressed: *Hypocrites! You are not interested in people! You care only for your own interests and have no heart for the one who is held a prisoner of evil:*

> "You hypocrites! Don't each of you untie your ox or donkey from the manger and lead it off to water on the Sabbath? Wasn't it proper for this daughter of Abraham, whom Satan had bound for these eighteen years, to be released from this bond on the Sabbath day?" (Lk 13:15–16; cf. Lk 6:6–10).

That woman was "bound"; Satan had kept her on a leash—"subjugated," as it were—with a heavy yoke that deformed the very body of the poor woman. This "daughter of Abraham" is now free; she has been "untied" by Jesus. And, not by chance, she has been healed on the Sabbath day, so that she can finally lift her gaze from the earth and contemplate heaven, glorifying God.

Luke rightly concludes that when Jesus "said these things, all his opponents were put to shame, and the whole crowd rejoiced at all the glorious things that were done by him" (Lk 13:17).

The forgiven woman

This is the last episode regarding a spiritual healing on which we would like to stop and reflect. We are once again inside a house. Jesus has accepted the invitation to dine at the house of a Pharisee, named Simon. He is reclining at a table with Simon and his friends. Everything seems to proceed normally, when all of a sudden an unexpected guest—or rather, an intruder—appears. It is a woman who is well known in the city for her infamous reputation:

There was a woman who was a sinner in the city, and when she learned that he was reclining at table in the Pharisee's house, she bought an alabaster jar of perfumed oil and stood by his feet, weeping, and she began to wet his feet with her tears and wipe them with the hair of her head, and she kissed his feet repeatedly and anointed them with the oil (Lk 7:37–38).

Simon's indignation is due less to the woman's behavior than to the Master's unseemly allowance of the action. The Pharisee does not have the courage to say openly what he is thinking, but if Jesus "were a prophet he would realize who and what kind of woman it is who is touching him..." (v. 39). Besides, his own reputation is at stake: he wants to show himself open and hospitable, but he doesn't deserve a scene like this in his house....

With his usual tact, Jesus intervenes to point out a truth in a sticky situation, showing authentic integrity and unmasking hypocrisy. He does not turn to the woman who is weeping at his feet, but to the one who had invited him to his house. Jesus addresses his host by name, with affection: "Simon, I have something to say to you." And the man responds graciously, hoping to fix an uncomfortable situation: "Speak, Teacher."

Jesus begins from a "safe distance," telling a parable:

"Two men were debtors of a certain money lender; the one owed five hundred denarii, the other, fifty. When they were unable to repay, he forgave them both. Which of them, then, will love him more?"

Simon lets himself be drawn in:

"I suppose the one he forgave the most."

Jesus agrees with him:

"You have judged correctly" (vv. 41–43).

Simon does not realize that he has just rendered judgment on himself. This very thing had happened to David ("You are that man!" cf. 2 Sam 12:1–7).

And like the prophet Nathan, Jesus too draws a conclusion at this point, making the woman's genuineness stand out sharply against the dull respectability of the Pharisee. Inviting Jesus to a meal, Simon was using the situation to his own advantage. He wanted to ingratiate himself with the Master, but without making enemies of the other rabbis, without upsetting the circle of Pharisees who were hostile to Jesus. Because of this he avoided everything that could compromise his position. He invited the Master but kept him at a certain distance, showing him no warmth:

> "You gave me no kisses, but she, from the moment she came in, has not stopped kissing my feet" (v. 45).

The people believed Jesus to be a prophet, and perhaps also for this reason Simon had invited him to his house. Now, one honors a prophet, but also simply an important guest, by pouring perfume on the person's head (cf. Ps 23: "my head you have anointed with oil"), something that Simon was well aware he should have done:

> "You did not anoint my head with olive oil, but she anointed my feet with perfumed oil" (v. 46).

Ultimately, Simon risked very little with his invitation. The woman, instead, risked her reputation, put her neck on the line. She had broken the rules by entering a place forbidden to her, such as a Pharisee's house, and immediately incurring the disdainful looks of those at table, their sharp judgment, and the weight of humiliation. She had not said a word, yet her behavior was unambiguous to the letter. Jesus understands the truth of her heart and defends her; she is a woman capable of great love:

> "Therefore I tell you: her sins, many as they are, have been forgiven, and so she has shown great love; but whoever is forgiven little, loves little" (v. 47).

Jesus addresses these words to Simon. Then, heedless of those present, he turns directly to the woman and pronounces words of interior healing:

> "Your sins are forgiven" (v. 48).

His table companions are scandalized and begin to say among themselves (like Simon, these men are also careful not to express themselves openly): "Who is this fellow who even forgives sins?" (v. 49) Jesus leaves them to their thoughts. His complete attention is for the woman crouched at his feet, whom he has fully forgiven of her many sins. For her he has one more word in store:

> "Your faith has saved you, go in peace!" (v. 50)

It is as if he were saying: Your great love for me is rooted in your faith; you have seen beyond and you have seen well. You have seen with the eyes of the heart. Go then toward peace (*eis eirenen*), in the certainty of pardon obtained.

The signs of the Gospel

In this chapter we have remembered several "miraculous healings": women healed in body and mind, women forgiven and transformed into disciples of the Lord. Wives, mothers, or daughters restored to the joy of life, to the joy of the whole family. The healing action of Jesus is a sign and confirmation of his Word. It is the Good News that brings salvation. The Gospel is truly strength for healing and the meaning of life. The Savior has come in fact to liberate man and woman, restoring health, dignity, and joy for service.

CHAPTER 10

The Gospel of Love

$\mathcal{T}$he Church has rediscovered the inseparable link between evangelization and the witness of charity, and she has committed herself to translating this into practice: "Charity is the privileged way of the 'new evangelization' so that, while it leads us to love humanity, it opens us to the encounter with God, the principal and the ultimate reason for every love." [5]

In this final *lectio,* dedicated to the theme of evangelization, we will dwell on the sixth chapter of Luke, the sublime section on the Beatitudes and on unconditional love, which must be open even to one's enemies. We will then go on to Luke 23, where these texts are completely fulfilled in the death of the Savior. Here we are invited to question ourselves on the truth of our love and on our

---

5. Italian Bishops' Conference, *Evangelizzazione e Testimonianza della Carità,* 1990.

capacity to extend this love even to our enemies, as the Gospel of Jesus asks us to do.

From the mountain to the plain

Like Moses, who descends from the top of the mountain with "the words of life" (cf. Ac 7:38), so Jesus descends with his disciples from the mountain where he has passed the night in prayer, and stops at a level place (Lk 6:17; an allusion to the plain where Israel encamped on the slopes of Sinai).

Jesus "descends" from the mountain to devote himself to healing suffering humanity. A great crowd is present, seeking spiritual and material help:

> When he came down with them he stood on a level place, and a large crowd of his disciples as well as a great number of the people from all Judea and Jerusalem and the coastal district of Tyre and Sidon came to hear him and be healed of their diseases, and those troubled by unclean spirits were cured. All the people kept trying to touch him, because power kept coming out from him and healing them all (Lk 6:17–19).

Luke places the Beatitudes and the discourse of love against this spacious backdrop: the level place is able to accommodate many people, something difficult to imagine on a mountaintop.

Beatitudes and woes

Luke 6:20–26 is told in two parts, paralleled with four beatitudes and four threats: a series of blessings and of warnings pronounced before a huge crowd. Yet, it is not specifically to the crowd that Jesus' eyes are directed. The people are undoubtedly there and they can hear, but it is to his disciples that Jesus looks, and it is to them that he turns in a direct way. In Matthew the Beatitudes are formulated in the third person ("Blessed are the poor, for theirs is the kingdom of heaven"); Luke, instead, uses the direct form ("Blessed are *you* poor, because *yours* is the Kingdom of God").

> "Blessed are you poor, for yours is the Kingdom of God.
> Blessed are you who hunger now, for you shall have your fill.
> Blessed are you who weep now, for you shall laugh.
> Blessed are you when men hate you" (vv. 20–22).

The word "blessed" appears in the Gospel of Luke fifteen times. The first time the word comes up, it refers to the Mother of Jesus, who is called "blessed" for having believed (Lk 1:45 and 1:48). The term "blessed" in Hebrew is *ashre,* and it recurs above all in the psalms and in the wisdom traditions (cf. Ps 1:1; 32:1–2; 41:2; 112:1; 119:1–2; 144:15; Prov 3:13; 8:32–34; Sir 14:1–2; 25:9; etc.).

A comparison of this text with Matthew shows some interesting aspects, whether regarding the structure or content of the passage. As has already been noted, Luke lists four beatitudes while Matthew offers eight. In Luke the blessings are contrasted with four warnings or threats, which are absent in Matthew. These are not interpreted as "curses" but as "warnings"—or, if necessary, as "laments"—in other words, we are not speaking of "blessing" the poor and "cursing" the rich! Rather, in continuity with biblical tradition, what is being explained here is the eschatological reasons of joy and, vice versa, of commiseration. The messianic age is in fact revealed because the poor, the hungry, and the sorrowful are worthy of the qualification of *makarioi*—blessed—and because the rich, the wise, and those who rejoice are, on the contrary, unfortunate.

Luke closely ties together the beatitudes of the poor and of those who are hungry, revealing in this a very concrete characteristic of poverty (evidenced in the parable of the poor Lazarus). On the other hand, being rich is associated with being happy: they are able to feast lavishly and to have no worry about what tomorrow may bring (evidenced by the reasoning of the rich man in Lk 12:16ff.). But those who rejoice now will experience the bitterness of tears, and those who are crying, great joy and liberating smiles (cf. Ps 126:1–3 and Rev 19:1–8). It is the same complete reversal of which the *Magnificat* sings (Lk 1:51–53).

In the first three blessings, the disciples are identified with the poor, the hungry, and those who are weeping, and are proclaimed "happy" because to them is announced the "Good News" of the coming of the reign of God. Their condition is under the sign of the cross. This follows closely Jesus' own life, signed with poverty (Lk 2:7; 9:58), hunger (freely choosing to enjoy "other bread": cf. Lk 4:2–4 and Deut 8:3), and tears (not of self-pity, but of bitterness for the rejection of Jerusalem: Lk 19:41–44 and 23:28).

The fourth beatitude describes further the Christological-ecclesial dimension. Not merely any suffering is rewarded, but the kind that is immensely blessed—"your reward is great in heaven"—is that which is for the sake of the Son of Man. Suffering for the sake of Christ follows the path already taken by the prophets (vv. 23 and 26) and witnesses to the steadfast person who accompanies the work of God in history (see Lk 11:47–50; 13:34f.).

Love of enemies

In continuity with the Beatitudes, Luke introduces a series of sayings on unconditional love, which is open also to one's enemies:

> "But to you who are listening, I say,
> Love your enemies,
> do good to those who hate you,
> bless those who curse you,
> pray for those who insult you.
> To the one who strikes you on one cheek,
> offer your other cheek as well,
> and from the one who takes your cloak,
> do not hold back your tunic" (Lk 6:27–29).

Love for one's enemies is the radical form of the commandment of love. The Law requires one to love one's *neighbor*, one's fellow human being, that is, whoever in various ways is connected to us by ties of family, race, culture, or religion. Those who study the Law limit themselves to asking, just as those who questioned Jesus, "Who is my neighbor?" And, consequently, "who has the right to benefit from my help?" Jesus decisively shifts one's understanding about the teaching of "being a neighbor." Every man or woman can become our "neighbor" if we want it so, if we move forward to encounter the other. From fraternity as an already-given reality, fruit of a closeness by ties of family, culture, or religion, Jesus goes on to point out the fraternity to be built through the free and gratuitous choice of "being a neighbor."

Jesus teaches us to allow an overflowing goodness toward all people to live in us; to offer love beyond the circle of relatives and friends, beyond the limits of race or nation, and even beyond the threshold of the community of faith. He teaches us *to be a neighbor, to become a fellow human being* even toward our enemies. This is the theme illustrated in the parable of the Good Samaritan, where the one who offers help to the unfortunate man attacked by bandits is a foreigner, someone different, one presumed to be an enemy. And it is precisely this man, the Samaritan, who, unlike the Levite and the priest, *makes himself* a neighbor by approaching the unhappy man, bending over him, tending his wounds, and taking care of him. In other words, Jesus is teaching us to construct fraternity through the free initiative of love, a love that impels us to "be a neighbor" to whoever has need of our help. "Go, and you do likewise" is the instruction that concludes the parable of the Good Samaritan (Lk 10:37). Solidarity is therefore the key to fraternity.

To do good is an unconditional absolute for the Rabbi of Nazareth, a fundamental duty that should be done in pure gratuitousness. It can't be compromised with waiting for a return: "If *you do good* to those who *do good to you,* what kindness is that in you? Even sinners do the same" (Lk 6:33).

In short, to do good to everyone, always, with detachment from self-interest and in sincere gratuitousness— behold the broad horizon placed before those who follow Jesus (cf. Lk 6:36–38). The Church has good reason, therefore, to propose charity as the obligatory way for the new evangelization. Only love, in fact, is worthy of faith:

> Evangelization is the witness of charity necessary today as the first step to accomplish; the growth of a Christian community which manifests in itself, through life and works, the Gospel of charity.[6]

The Gospel of love on the cross

Jesus not only taught love toward one's enemies; above all he lived it in an extraordinary way. His death is a witness of disconcerting meekness. Jesus does not ask for vengeance, does not make himself the interpreter of God's justice at the supreme moment of his crucifixion, unlike the Maccabee brothers, who reminded their executioners that they would not escape the divine judgment (2 Mac 7:16, 34–36). Jesus, instead, dies asking forgiveness for his persecutors (Lk 23:34). In this way he does not allow himself to be caught up in the spiral of violence, but overcomes evil with good, forgiving his enemies, just as he had taught his followers to do (Lk 6:27–29).

---

6. Ibid., no. 26.

We place ourselves beneath the cross of the Lord. Luke refers to three groups of scoffers. In this he is in agreement with Mark. What is different are the protagonists. Luke does not speak of passersby who scoff at the end of the alleged Messiah. The people, who are already present at the scene, are not associated with those who are jeering; they stand and watch in silence. The three groups are made up of the leaders of the people, the soldiers, and one of the two criminals who were crucified to the right and left of Jesus. These three groups follow one after the other in a hammering demand: "Save yourself."

> The rulers made fun of him, saying, "He saved others, let him save himself, if this fellow is God's Messiah..." (Lk 23:35).
>
> The soldiers...also mocked him, offering him sour wine and saying, "If you are the King of the Jews, save yourself" (v. 37).
>
> One of the criminals who was hanging blasphemed him and said, "Are you not the Messiah? Save yourself and us!" (v. 39)

The sarcasm emanating from the three groups is the same. Their statements all contain two parts, one hypothetical (If you are the Christ...) and the other imperative (save yourself!). Variations exist, but the theme is always that of being the Messiah ("If you are the Christ...; if you are the King of the Jews"), connected with the act of saving. From the Messiah one expects acts of salvation. The prerogative of the Christ is to be a Savior.

This is seen above all in the Gospel of Luke. Announcing the birth of Jesus, the angels say to the shepherds: "Today is born for you a Savior, who is Christ the Lord" (Lk 2:11). The three sarcastic statements are therefore a challenge, or, rather, a triple temptation (see Lk 4:1–13: "If you are the Son of God..."). While Jesus responded unfailingly to the tempter in the desert at the beginning of his ministry, here on the cross he remains silent. And so the challenge lies open: if Jesus does not work signs of salvation, how can anyone be expected to recognize such a "Messiah"?

Against this dramatic background, Luke places the dialogue with the good thief (who is actually never called such by Luke). The thief begins by disassociating himself from the derisive scorn uttered by his companion in crime. "But the other rebuked him and said, 'Do you not fear God?'" (Lk 23:40)

Other translations vary somewhat: "Not even you are afraid of God?" letting it be understood that, like the leaders and the soldiers, even the criminals are demonstrating they are not afraid of God. But the negative *oudé* is connected to the verb "to be afraid" and not to the pronoun "you." The meaning therefore seems to be the following: *You have not been afraid of man and so you have arrived at this end, but don't you even have a fear of God? You could at least have that!* (This is seen in the parable of the judge, who is neither afraid of God nor has respect for men: see Lk 18:1ff.)

Then the thief recognizes his culpability, telling his companion that while their punishment is deserved, that of Jesus is unjust: "...you are under the same sentence! And we justly, for we are being paid back fittingly for what we did, while this fellow has done nothing wrong" (v. 41).

And so the innocence of Jesus is again proclaimed, and precisely by the one who was designated as a "criminal." After Jesus' death, this innocence will be recognized also by the centurion (23:47). In the account of Acts it will become like a refrain: Jesus is innocent, he did no evil (Ac 2:22; 3:13; 7:52; 22:14).

The recognition of the thief's own guilt and, at the same time, of the innocence of Jesus are what constitute then a "true confession" that opens him to salvation. It is never too late. Jesus saves even those who, like the repentant thief, turn to him at the last moment. He is the Savior full of goodness. And this is the prayer of the good thief: "...Jesus, remember me when you come into your Kingdom" (v. 42).

This extreme confidence is surprising. The repentant criminal turns to Jesus, calling him by name. This is the only time we find the name "Jesus" invoked without any accompanying title; the only time in the whole New Testament. What does this prayer express? Undoubtedly a great hope. The newly converted man recognizes the messianic royalty of Jesus and he entrusts himself to it. His prayer lets us understand that he waits for the messianic coming at the end of time, in the future coming of God, when Jesus will manifest himself as Savior.

Jesus' response is prompt and solemn: "Amen, I say to you, this day you will be with me in Paradise" (v. 43). The good thief had asked "when...," and Jesus responds:

"Today!" It is the today of salvation, which runs through the whole Gospel of Luke: today is born for you a Savior (2:11); today this Scripture is fulfilled in your hearing (4:20); today salvation has come to this house (19:9).

What does this response, so full of sovereign authority, actually mean? Jesus, who kept silent before the taunting of the leaders, the soldiers, and the impenitent thief, offers to this poor man a response that far surpasses his request. Not tomorrow, but today; not a simple remembrance ("remember me"), but a promise to be with Jesus: "You will be with me in Paradise." The penitent asked for a future liberation. Jesus offers him salvation today.

What kind of salvation? Not one that eliminates suffering and death, but one that is accomplished through suffering and death. In this way Jesus reveals himself as the Messiah who saves. His way of being Christ the Savior is not accomplished by saving *from* suffering and death, but by saving *in* suffering and death.

Which salvation are we to proclaim?

Luke's presentation of the death of Jesus leads us spontaneously to ask ourselves which ministry of salvation the Church is called to develop. How does the Church, which is called to be for all humanity "a sign and sacrament of salvation" (*Lumen Gentium,* no. 1) accomplish her ministerial duty?

A recurring temptation is to enact a model of misleading service that shuns the cross. Whoever uses a more or less magical power to "save" oneself or others from the cross adopts the same way of seeing as the leaders, the soldiers, and the impenitent thief. This is certainly not the way Jesus sees, and therefore is not even Christian.

On the other hand, the announcement of a salvation that refers only to the end of the world, when God will wipe away "every tear" (Rv 7:17), may resemble the good thief's way of seeing, but it is still considered insufficient by Jesus.

The salvation that the Crucified promises is not only a salvation for tomorrow, it already permeates today.

To conclude with the words of J. Dupont:

> Jesus himself invites his companion in torture to conceive a profound faith, one capable of recognizing God's salvific presence in that which is the most scandalous negation of it, that is, in the suffering of the innocent.... Jesus' response to the good thief says clearly that God is present, even today, there where one suffers and dies for the cause of justice, peace, and the unity of the human race. In the cross God shows that love is stronger than death, that the secret of salvation resides in the value of the cross: as the revelation of the God who saves. This is the most precious and urgent ministry there is today, that is awaited even by Christians.[7]

---

7. "Gesù Salvatore," in *Parole de vita,* 36 (1991), 277.

Prayer to continue the journey

*L*ord Jesus,
we believe that you have conquered death
and have made life flourish.
But during the journey
we sometimes feel disappointed and dismayed.
As the two travelers on the road to Emmaus,
we struggle to understand the meaning
of sadness, of humiliation, and of death—
yours, Lord, and ours.
The sacred texts and history remained
"closed" to us,
closed with seven seals....
Only you could take the book
and break open the seals,
O immolated Lamb!
Reveal to us, then, the meaning of Scripture,
the meaning of human suffering and death.
Teach us the love that is stronger than death.
Stay with us.
May our eyes be opened and recognize you.
Let us leave without delay,
and we will raise the world to a new hope:
The Lord is indeed risen!